D1871270

# THE STORY OF FORT ST. GEORGE

# THE STORY OF FORT ST. GEORGE

BY

COL. D. M. REID

O.B.E., M.C., E.D., A.D.C.

ILLUSTRATED BY

ISMENA R. WARREN

WITH A FOREWORD BY

H. E. SIR ARTHUR HOPE

G.C.I.E., M.C.

GOVERNOR OF MADRAS

DIOCESAN PRESS

MADRAS

1945

GOVERNMENT HOUSE
Ootacamund,
7th June 1945.

Everyone who has had the good fortune, as I have, to be conducted on a tour round the Fort by Colonel Reid will be delighted that he has set down his unequalled knowledge and his enthusiastic love of the Fort in such extremely readable form.

Colonel Reid is a South Indian enthusiast and his work is all the better for his enthusiasm for whether one agrees with him or not—and I personally consider that his claims for the achievements of South Indian troops are not in the least exaggerated—his enthusiasm gives him the power of enlivening the pages of history and of making the streets, walls and buildings of the Fort themselves tell their enthralling tale.

The story of Fort St. George is in epitome, the story of the British connection with India, and Colonel Reid is obviously proud of it. He may justly be proud not only of the story of the Fort, but also of his achievement in setting it down in a manner which will earn for him the gratitude of many.

Arthur Hope

GOVERNOR OF MADRAS

# CONTENTS

# THE STORY OF FORT ST. GEORGE

Francis Day offered to bet Andrew Cogan that a sandy strip between the Cooum River and the sea was worth having as a settlement for the East India Company. He had just been there and had returned up the Coast, having made an agreement with the local Rajah. That was in 1639 when Charles I was King of England.

**A Wager**

'Changes of time are fickle,' he said, 'and if you suffer this opportunity to pass over, you shall perhaps in vain afterwards pursue the same when it is fled and gone.'

On that strip of land are now the historic buildings of Fort St. George, Madras. Many a traveller arrives at the railway station almost within sight of it, goes to a hotel, canteen or hostel not far away, and 'suffers the opportunity to pass over', the opportunity to spare an hour to see the ground and buildings where Clive and Wellington made history and where, indeed, an Empire was founded.

History often seems such a dull subject, but when it is put over in a cinema film it becomes well and acceptable. Why not go and see a living film? The houses and streets, the Church and the Mess, the silver plate and the old registers, the ramparts and the moats, create to anyone with imagination a living picture, with shades rustling their laces and ruffles, wearing wigs or crinolines, and the sound can almost be heard of many a pipe of madeira wine rumbling down Snobs' Alley.

The best preliminary to a visit to the Fort is to spread out the eight maps contained at the end of this book, and to run through the story.

The tale started before the British came here. Legend has it that St. Thomas, the Apostle, brought Christianity to India, and was martyred at St. Thomas' Mount, which is about 8 miles from Fort St. George. Certainly in the year A.D. 800 Arabs called the village of San Thomé 'Bar Thoma', or the 'Town of Thomas'. King Alfred of England sent a gift to the shrine of St. Thomas.

**St. Thomas**

In 1522 the Portuguese occupied San Thomé, which is now a suburb of Madras, about 4 miles south of the Fort. That was when Henry VIII was King of England, when the English were too busy with other things to think much about the East Indies.

**The Portuguese**

The Portuguese had a good start, and got a strong hold on the trade in spices and cotton goods. In those days in Europe, food was not so appetising as it is today. Potatoes had not yet been introduced from Peru. Men usually ate their meat with nothing other than their dagger and a piece of bread. Wheat was, of course, ground into flour, and we hear of venison pasties, but there cannot have been much variety of vegetables inside the pasty.

Mustard was grown in England, but there was no pepper, except when it was bought at a great price from the Portuguese who had imported it from India. We are apt to forget today what an important part spices play in our food.

The art of delicate eating had been forgotten for 1,200 years, ever since the Roman Empire was overrun by the barbarians. The Romans knew how to prepare appetising food, but they had outposts all over the known world, and, indeed, had a cohort at Calicut, on the West Coast of South India. There can be little doubt that they got their pepper. That cohort, or company of infantry, was not there for nothing.

In the period about which we are talking, 1522 to 1600, the clothes that people wore in England, in the reigns of Henry VIII and Elizabeth, were made of wool. The rich people had also silk and linen, but the poor could not afford those expensive fabrics, and therefore had no underclothes at all. Cotton did not start being produced in America for a long time yet. The main source of cotton goods was India, and particularly South India. It can be understood that cotton goods were eagerly sought.

During the sixteenth century there were two main difficulties about getting cotton fabrics and pepper. The Portuguese exacted an enormous profit on the goods in which they traded, making them very expensive, and there were constant outbreaks of war to upset the trade. Besides which, no nation likes to be at the mercy of another, and to see the whole of a trade in the hands of another country.

British merchants got tired of it, and decided to do something. A group of men in London got together and founded a company to trade in the East. They obtained a charter from Queen Elizabeth, and that was the beginning of the famous East India Company, in the year 1600.

**The Company**

The Dutch had the same idea, and so had the French and the Danes.

It was a long voyage, in small sailing ships, often not larger than 300 tons, all the way round the Cape of Good Hope to India, in the face of enemies of all kinds, wind, weather and human, not to speak of the troubles of food and water supply.

In 1612 the East India Company started business at Surat, about 150 miles north of Bombay. Later, in 1616, they came round to the eastern side of India and opened up at Masulipatam. They came further south to Armagon, north of Pulicat in 1626, but had not yet got proper access to the cotton trade of South India. The Portuguese and the Dutch still controlled the important trade in calicoes, long-cloths, muslins and chintzes.

Francis Day was therefore on to something important when he came further south and negotiated a treaty with the Rajah of Chandragiri for an establishment of the English Company in his dominions. More important still, for the first time, the Company was going to own territory in India, and was to fortify it. In the other places they merely had offices and trading posts.

It took them 13 years to build the small fort shown in this map. The Rajah promised to give assistance, but did not do so. It probably started as a palisade and was gradually built up with stone, earth and brick. The sea and the river are in blue. The houses are marked in red. It will be noticed that a few buildings had grown up to the North of the Fort.

**Map I. 1653**

The outline of today's Fort is superimposed in black dotted lines, so that the comparative location can be seen.

It will be noticed that the Secretariat, marked

Now turn to Map VIII

'A' the seat of the Government of Madras today, occupies exactly the site of Francis Day's first Fort. Note that the river originally ran through the site of the present Fort. The edge of the present barrack square, marked 'B', was then river.

All round were low sandy dunes. In the distance were small collections of fishermen's huts, near a few palm trees. Catamarans untied, and loose in their separate logs gleamed white in the sun. The early morning scene must have been very like

CATAMARANS

what it is on the coast twenty or thirty miles from Madras today Let us picture two English sailors, Thomas King and David Rogers, tramping over the sand in the year 1653.

They are led by a group of three Indians, and wade slowly through the river in the direction of Yerramboor village (Egmore), to fetch and escort back some cart-loads of rice. The Englishmen placidly accept the discomfort of the rough woollen breeches and coats which they wear, in the same way as Europeans have submitted to clothes of dignity ever since. Their wide-brimmed hats shade their eyes from the sun.

They walk in silence until King says to Rogers : Will you go to Meliapore (Mylapore) tonight?'

'What is that to you?' asks Rogers.

'The fair Maria Fonseca will be waiting for you.'

'And what if she is?' grunts Rogers more irritably.

'Nothing, but I have a fancy that William Smith may find his way there tonight.'

The argument, gossip and confidences follow in the way that they have for three hundred years since then. Rogers married Maria, and William married her sister. The two men, like as not, died in the country, and their descendants, named Rogers and Smith, are here today.

Twenty years pass. The settlement has increased. Houses in compounds have been built alongside the river, godowns to the North of the old Fort, a wall round three sides, and a village has grown up to the North.

**Map II. 1673**

In the vacant spaces in the extended fortification thatched huts cover dwellings and accumulations of merchandise of the rougher sort, skins and hides half-tanned, carpenters making furniture or working for ships, carts being mended, cattle feeding from coarse forage.

Out at sea, in the Roads off the sandy beach, two

small ships ride at anchor facing the prevailing southerly breeze. A masula boat, fashioned in the same way as today with planks sewn together with coir twine, and caulked with coconut fibre, paddles slowly towards the breakers, bringing a barrel ashore for water. It reaches the surf, chooses its moment and comes riding in to bump elastically on to the sand bar, up again and over smoother water to reach the shore.

David Roger's son, Samuel, a fine young man, shouts in fluent Tamil, asking if they have brought

Bringing Goods Ashore

the big saw from the ship. Gesticulation cover their explanations. Misunderstanding of instructions occurred not for the first time in this country Time marches on.

'About this date, in 1672, a young man named Elihu Yale, arrived out in Madras to serve the Company. He had been born at Boston, in the New England colony of Massachusetts, in 1649, but his father, for some reason or other, brought the famliy back to England when Elihu was still only a small boy.

**Elihu Yale**

At the age of 23, Elihu obtained employment from the Company, sailed to India and made good progress in Madras where he gradually made a fortune. The Company's servants, in those days, all took part in private trading, as well as attending to the Company's business. At the age of 28, he joined with the others in the Fort in supporting the scheme for building a Church. The Governor, Streynsham Master, realised that the Directors in London would not be likely to favour spending money on such a commercially unprofitable project. The Company was only interested in profits and dividends. Streynsham Master does not appear to have consulted the Directors at all. He was the sort of man who did not disobey orders; he acted without them. He went ahead in his ideas about a Church, and collected money from private subscribers, one of whom was Elihu Yale who paid 15 pagodas. The Church was designed and built by Edward Fowle, the Master Gunner of the Fort. In those days the gunners were also the engineers. St. Mary's Church took two years to build, and was duly consecrated on Lady Day 1680. It is thus the oldest English Church in Asia.

In 1687 Yale became Governor, at the age of 39.

He ordered from England a handsome silver alms-dish which he presented to the Church. This may be seen in the Chaplain's house today.

After five years he was replaced by Sir John Goldsborough, who presented a silver flagon and basin to the Church, which may also be seen. The basin fits into the front in the Church and is used for christenings

**Goldsborough**

Governor Yale eventually retired to London where his great wealth attracted attention. In America, far across the Atlantic, stories of his affluence came to the ears of the Rev. James Pierpont, Principal of the Collegiate School at Saybrook, not far from Boston, who, no doubt, discussed it with old-timers who remembered the Yale family.

Pierpont was a man of action. He seized the opportunity and wrote a 'proper' letter to Elihu Yale, describing the achievements and aspirations of the College. The result was that Yale sent between 30 and 40 volumes of books for the college library. Two years later the trustees of the school decided to remove it from Saybrook to Newhaven. They started building boldly, and made considerable progress, but soon exhausted their funds. They wrote again to Yale, asked for his charity and proposed that the college should have his valuable name. Yale responded by sending them three trunks of valuable goods in a vessel bound for Boston, to be sold for the benefit of the college. The goods produced £800, which was the largest sum that the College had ever received from a private person. The buildings were completed and the name Yale began to mean something in education. That is the story of the

**Yale University**

early days of the great and world-famous University of Yale.

By 1710 Fort St. George had filled up with proper houses, a considerable town had resulted on the northern side. Observe that the Church, marked with a white cross in the map, just to the south of the inner old fort, now shows in the map. The alignments of most of the streets in this map are the same today The blocks of buildings were in reality divided into many different houses, often privately owned, but the divisions between them are nowhere now on record. In general the houses on the northern side were private, while those to the south belonged to the Company. The town outside the Fort to the north, with an Indian population, was laid out in streets and was fairly well organised. The narrow space between the northern wall of the Fort and the houses of the town was known as the Parade Ground. During the day this was the market place. Along the line of houses facing the Fort was a row of shops. Married soldiers were allowed to live in the town behind the shops, and went into the Fort every day, through the two gates—the Choultry gate (now bricked up), and North Gate.

**Map III. 1710**

Here during the morning ladies from the Fort would meet their friends and do their marketing while their husbands were busy near the sea gate with newly landed goods, or working in the offices of the Company. Each lady would be accompanied by two or three servants, cheerful chattering creatures, and by her palanquin bearers. The bustling scene must have been very like what it is today in Georgetown, except that European costumes were different. Indian bazaar houses have changed very little with the passing of years. At each little stall the vendors sat and waved away the

Shopping in Blacktown 1814

flies, showed their wares, and argued the price, fanam by fanam or cash by cash.

Portuguese ladies were in evidence, just as Anglo-Indians are today. The Portuguese Settlement of San Thomé had been taken over by the British in 1675, and many Portuguese had forsaken Meliapore (now Mylapore) to come and live in 'Gentoo' town ('Gentoo' is the same as the modern 'Hindu'). These ladies mingled with the English ladies and discussed their children's ailments or the likelihood of a new arrival for some post by the next ship. Appointments and promotions, retirements and injustices were always a matter for gossip and argument, as they have been ever since.

The common language of the market at that time was Portuguese, mixed with Tamil and English. The descendants of the many Company's English soldiers who married Eurasian or Indian women were all brought up to speak English as their mother-tongue, and so the Portuguese speech gradually disappeared. It is interesting to note that large numbers of Portuguese and Anglo-Indians served in the Company's European regiment, which had been started in 1668.

Another interesting feature is that the Portuguese and Anglo-Indian ladies wore the Spanish and Portuguese black lace mantilla over the head, which custom continued until comparatively recent times.

The period about which we are speaking, around the year 1710, was notable for the building of the Egmore Redoubt, a small Fort which stood until recent years near the present Egmore Station. Many living people will remember it. It was pulled down to make room for quarters for the South Indian Railway employees.

The S.P.C.K., a missionary society, in 1711 sent out to Tranquebar a printer and a printing press.

**Printing**

The work gradually expanded. Later, at the fall of Pondicherry, in 1760 a printing press was brought from there to Madras and presented to the Society on condition that it should be at the service of the Government if required. From such beginnings grew the great Diocesan Press of today.

Missionaries now played a considerable part in the development of cultural life in the Fort and surroundings. Most of the missionaries were recruited from the university of Halle, in Germany, and were sent out under the inspiration of the King of Denmark. They were good Christian men, loyal to the Company, and were often the only chaplains available. Schwartz was one of these.

**Map IV 1746**

The period through which we pass between 1710 and 1746 was one of steadily increasing trade, but was also, like other periods of our history, under a continual threat of war. When the Fort was first founded the Company had only to face attack from one or more of conflicting Hindu parties. It had several sieges of a minor nature. Later, the Mahommedan power from the North of India came down to the South, and the political situation changed, though not towards more enduring peace. Added to this the French were at Pondicherry. Whenever England was at war with France in Europe, it followed that the Company in Madras was at war with the French at Pondicherry.

The matter of the defence of the Fort was one of deep concern, but it was difficult to convince the Board of Directors in London that the large sums of money required to be spent on it were really necessary. Out here in Madras, it was quite clear that the western face was weak, and that the jumble of houses to the north of the Fort was masking the guns and would give excellent cover for an enemy's attack. The river to the west of the Fort looks broad and a sufficient obstacle on the map, but in reality it must have been fordable anywhere, and no obstacle at all.

Various plans were put up and argued without much result. It must be remembered that throughout the long life of the Company there was only one object, the legitimate object of any trading concern, the payment of dividends. The Directors in London looked with disfavour or anything like conquest, or militarism. What they really liked were nice satisfying treaties where the eventual results could be calculated and assessed by accountants. They realised that other things had to be done, money—a little—had to be spent on a chaplain, or on educating children, and to a certain extent on building expensive ramparts and furnishing them with cannon, powder and shot. The European Regiment of the Company gradually grew by an extra battalion at a time. Ships had to be furnished and manned. But behind it all the annual Profit and Loss Account was what really mattered.

As 1746 approached defences had been built on the west side of the river, and there had been a certain amount of clearance of the houses outside the northern ramparts, but the work was nothing like what the experts on the spot demanded.

The year 1739 was a fateful one in Europe. Prosperous England forced Walpole to declare war on Spain. The struggle for Empire between France and Britain started and continued with brief interruptions for 75 years.

In South India there were two claimants for the throne of the Nawab of the Carnatic. France supported one, the English the other. Therefore, whether England and France were at war or not, they were perpetually, if unofficially, at war in South India.

**Robert Clive**

Into this atmosphere came a youth of 18, Robert Clive, in the year 1743. Born at Market Drayton, in Shropshire, he had led a turbulent early life, and was sent out to India as being the best thing for him, in the appointment of 'Writer', the junior covenanted rank in the service of the Company. From the beginning he did not take to the office desk at all. Copying out letters in a legible hand, adding up pagodas, fanams and cash, checking the contents of bales and trunks was to him utter boredom. He saw one avenue of escape. His friends in the Company's European Regiment, had a much better time than he did, and they did not seem to be prevented from making money by private trading from time to time. He saw that he would be far happier if he could have a commission as Ensign in the regiment. He therefore applied and waited. Red tape and delays seem always to have existed. Soldiers of today need not think that the necessary delay of a few weeks, in dealing with an application, is a hardship. In those days delays were figured in years. Indeed things were much worse then, when the junior was very much the junior and was kept in his place with very little consideration for his feelings or desires.

Clive must have walked round the ramparts in the comparative cool of many an evening, brooding alone. The breakers of the Bay of Bengal crashed onto the sand twenty yards away from the eastern walls of the Fort. Uneducated sweat-laden soldiers, often recruited and brought out from the gaols of London, cleaned cannon or carried up stores from the vaults of the ramparts where many of them lived. Barrack accommodation hardly existed at all. Amenities consisted of the arrack shops of Blacktown (to the North of the Fort) or walks to the disorderly purlieus of Hog Hill which stood near where the Central Station platforms now stretch, 'a resort for licentious soldiers by night'.

Clive borrowed books and read, and brooded. His attempts to enter the Company's army seemed heavy with failure. The heat was oppressive. Or the long rains of the monsoon season kept him to the house where he was ill-tempered to his friends and unsociable.

It is said that one day he decided to take his life. He put the pistol to his head and pressed the trigger. It misfired.

Behind the cover of his moody temperament fancies formed themselves into pictures of his imagination, of a girl perhaps that he remembered in Market Drayton. His repression could not altogether subdue his longing to talk to someone with whom he need not be on the defensive, someone who would understand his hopes and ambitions. Like many another young man, far from home, he built up an ideal, which returned to him when he was alone, or perhaps when a day-dream possessed him as he sat at a table sorting lists and invoices of goods. Rolls of broadcloth from England in different colours were detailed in front of him, with separate entries for each shipment to which they belonged. They faded and came into perspective as he frowned and forced himself back to his work.

Not far away was another young writer, Edmund Maskelyne. They had nothing particularly in common. Edmund was slow and deliberate, taking things very much as they came. He felt no particular grievances against anyone or anything in particular, was obedient to authority, and joined cheerfully with other young men in the coffee-house or tavern.

One day Clive looked in at a room to see Edmund arranging some of his possessions. His eye caught a small picture, a miniature of a girl. As Edmund turned away, Clive started at it, and stood motionless. Edmund looked round and said :

'What ails you, Robert?'

'Nothing', replied Clive. His moods were nothing new to Maskelyne, who shrugged his shoulders, and asked :

'Is it trouble at the Counting House or what?'

Clive turned away without replying.

'A strange fellow', muttered Maskelyne, not worrying, and went on with what he was doing.

Clive probably said nothing for some days. Then he approached Maskelyne and asked to see the miniature. Edmund, as like as not, laughed and said:

'And you Robert added to her list? Odds body, you'll have to call out both Cornelius and Fordyce in turn, for they swear their hearts are hers.'

Clive & the miniature

Clive was a very determined man when his mind was set. The first principle of war was always clear in his mind, the 'Maintenance of the Object'. There can be little doubt that he replied amicably, for he could control himself well when he had an object. From that moment he cultivated Maskelyne, and probably paid his respects to his aunt Elizabeth, who was the widow of Joseph Walsh who died in 1731, and whose tomb-stone can be seen in the pavement round St. Mary's Church.

His ambition now had a clear task, to make himself a quick fortune and sail back to England, a remote possibility indeed in the low position which he held, and in his dislike of trade, or he would make himself famous and she would come out to him.

The miniature remained a guiding light during the violent and intense activities of the next five years.

In the growing threats from the French, and in the certainty that something would happen soon, he saw relief from his restricted occupation and his chance. It came.

News of the outbreak of war between England and France reached Madras in September 1744.

**French in the Fort**

The English fleet had arrived off the Fort in August, and might have attacked Pondicherry, but the monsoon was approaching, and the fleet sailed away to Sumatra.

A French fleet under Admiral de lo Bourdonnais then arrived. It had an indecisive engagement with part of the English fleet which was dispersed. The French Admiral went to Pondicherry, and the English might reasonably have thought that nothing would happen until after the monsoon. But the French General, Dupleix, insisted on an attack on Madras. On 3rd September 1746 the French fleet appeared off Madras and landed troops near the present Examination Hall of the University. Batteries were set up on the banks of the Cooum, and the ships also bombarded the Fort from the sea. In three days the Fort capitulated. Clive was taken prisoner with the rest of the Company's forces and servants. The French held Fort St. George for three years, during which they proceeded with the clearance of the houses to the north of the Fort up to the present alignment of the Esplanade, which runs from Parry's Building westwards.

Clive escaped and made his way to Fort St. David, Cuddalore, which is somewhat to the south

**Ensign Clive**

of Pondicherry. There he joined the forces as a volunteer and distinguished himself greatly. As a result he was granted his commission as an Ensign, and he was very well reported on to the Directors. In a letter from London they order: 'Be sure to encourage Ensign Clive in his Martial Pursuits. According to his Merit, any improvement he shall make shall be duly regarded by us.' This meant that the Board in London were prepared to approve of further promotion. Edmund Maskelyne was given a commission at the same time.

Clive fought well round Pondicherry, but had a quarrel with a brother officer which nearly resulted in a duel. Clive was undoubtedly the injured party, and behaved well. In 1749 he was appointed Quartermaster.

Clive's commission was really only a temporary one. When peace with France was announced in Europe as a result of the Treaty of Aix-la-Chapelle, the news in India resulted in Fort St. George being handed back to the Company by the French. Clive saw no further promise of active service, so resigned his commission. He returned to civil work in the Company's service.

**Fort returned**

Thus the end of 1749 sees the Fort back in British hands. But it was not to be peace for long, for the 'War of the Coromandel' started in 1750. Clive was then Steward at Fort St. David. The dispute between two opposing rulers, Chanda Sahib and Muhammad Ali flared up in the Carnatic, aggravated by the uncertain attitudes of the Mahrattas and the Nizam. The French and the British were, of course, on opposite sides. Muhammad Ali, supported by the British, found himself besieged in Trichinopoly where heavy fighting took place.

In order to relieve Trichinopoly, a diversion was arranged with Clive to lead it. He had returned to

Military service, and was made a captain, at the age of 27. He returned to Madras and was given all the Europeans out of the Fort garrison except 50 men. He marched out with his force of 200 Europeans, 300 Sepoys, and 8 young officers, half of whom were civil servants.

As they slowly made their way along the well-known road, through Poonamallee going westwards, with the dim Nagari Hills in the far distance on their right, it may be that they left something in the atmosphere to encourage their grandsons whose trucks and lorries rolled along this road so often two centuries later. The graves in the cemeteries all along the route tell of what they went through with exhaustion, disease, dirt and privations, at a time when there was no aspirin, no iodine, no comforts, no chlorine and no one knew that water should be boiled. Nor was anyone inoculated, and their uniforms were not designed for tropical comfort. When they marched they were accompanied by a wonderfully varied train of animals, carts and wagons, palanquins borne by four or more bearers, and their cannon were drawn by bullocks. Their food was mainly collected on the way, and paid for in actual coin. Silver and gold were taken with the force for that purpose, pagodas, rupees, fanams and cash. There were many different types of coin, of varying fineness, so that every payment seems to have been a matter for argument. The gold pagoda, a small gold coin slightly larger than the front end of the modern collar-stud, was worth from 3 to 3½ silver rupees. Each rupee was equal to about 12 fanams, each of which were equal to 80 cash.

The coinage was first standardized in 1741 when

the Company issued their famous gold Star Pagoda.

**Coinage**

We may take it that the coinage was more or less as below :—

| *Old Coinage* | | *Modern Money* |
|---|---|---|
| 1 pagoda | ... | 3 rupees |
| 1 rupee | ... | 1 rupee |
| 1 fanam | ... | 1 anna 4 pies |
| 1 cash | ... | One-fifth of a pie |

Besides these there were crowns, dollars, mohurs, pieces-of-eight and other coins of many different nations, which were worth whatever was the value of the gold or silver inside them. It was all very complicated. All paymasters must have been very patient men.

Clive marched on and occupied Arcot without opposition. It came as a surprise and a shock to the French and their Indian allies, and, as was intended, caused a diversion from Trichinopoly. Clive was himself, before long besieged in Arcot. He had repaired the fortifications as much as he could in the time available, and faced the surrounding masses with his small force. A well-known story tells how the seige lasted until the food was down to almost nothing, and that the sepoys voluntarily gave their rice to the European soldiers, retaining for themselves only the water in which the rice had been boiled, because they felt that they could keep going on that but the Europeans couldn't.

**Siege of Arcot**

The story of the siege of 50 days is one of unparalleled leadership and example. At one critical moment, when a large raft containing a mass of the enemy's swordsmen and spearmen was crossing the moat, Clive himself trained a cannon at very close range and fired it, destroying the raft and all on it.

This siege took up so much of the enemy's time and men, and its continuance was so impressive that it had its effect on the general morale of the whole

of the enemy's forces. When Clive's garrison was eventually relieved by a detachment under Capt. Kilpatrick, Clive took the field in other directions, had successes at Arnee and Conjeeveram and, at last, returned to Madras.

The result of all this was that the whole attitude of South India towards the British rapidly changed. Up to that time the French had been greatly respected for their military prowess, but the English were considered inferior. Clive's defence of Arcot came at the right time and has been well described as the turning point in British History in India.

Just about that time Major Stringer Lawrence, another famous Madras name, arrived back from

England as Commander-in-Chief. He went off at once to Trichinopoly, supported by Clive and fought the war to a finish.

Clive was back in the Fort in 1752 as Steward. His friendship with Edmund Maskelyne had continued, and they had no doubt discussed with Mrs. Elizabeth Walsh the idea of her niece Margaret making the journey out to Madras. Clive had never wavered from his devotion to the miniature of Margaret. They weighed up all the dangers and difficulties of the long voyage, and read eagerly the letters from home replying to what Clive had urged Edmund to write. It must have covered a period of years, for letters took anything from four to perhaps eight months in transit. British women did come out on the long journey in those days, braving all that small sailing ships, contrary winds, storms, failing provisions and cramped quarters meant.

**Clive as Steward**

In 1753 Margaret arrived. Clive may have heard of the name of her ship, for letters sometimes came on ahead by a fast sailer. The postal route overland via Bombay and Suez and later via 'Bussorah' (Basrah) had not yet begun. It started about 1790.

How long Miss Margaret Maskelyne was in Madras before Clive proposed is not known. Reserved as he was, he was determined. On the 18th of February 1753, they were married in St. Mary's Church by the Reverend Mr. Fabricius, a Danish Missionary, who was officiating after the sad death of the Company's Chaplain.

**Clive's Marriage**

The marriage was a very happy one, the one happy and contented thing in Clive's vivid and brilliant career. Though he was so outstanding and did so much for the Company and for his country, and though he eventually amassed a great fortune, he suffered in health and in spirits, and, when he finally retired to England from Bengal in 1765 he was fiercely attacked for the remaining years of his life by jealous and critical enemies. Jealousy is really the root of all evil, another word for which is 'envy'.

Clive was in ill-health in 1752, before his marriage, and had applied for special leave home. He got it and sailed with his wife in 1753. This was unusual in those days, especially with one so young as he was. A man's service usually continued uninterruptedly until he retired and went home with his fortune, or died and was buried in the cemetery which lay where the Law College Buildings now stand. Clive wisely went home in time, and recuperated. He was lucky. Most men were not able to do that.

**39th Foot**

In 1754 the first King's Regiments to arrive in India came out with a squadron of the Royal Navy under Rear-Admiral Watson and eventually arrived at Fort St. George. It was the Thirty-Ninth Foot, Adlercron's Regiment. This today is the First Battalion of the Dorsetshire Regiment, whose proud motto tells of this arrival in Madras, *Primus in Indis*. With it came a detachment of the Royal Artillery. This was the beginning of military assistance to the Company by Parliament.

**Reconstruction of Fort**

The new design for rebuilding the Fort was accepted and had been started when the 39th arrived. They were probably first accommodated in various parts of the Fort and in huts outside, since the Fort itself

must have been full of coolies and workmen, and littered with stacks of bricks and building material. The North and South curtains (straight walls) were not altered much, but the whole western face started on a complete transformation.

King's Barracks and the Guardroom were under construction. The 39th were their first occupants.

In 1755 Clive returned as Deputy-Governor of Fort St. David, Cuddalore, after having been very well treated in England. The Company honoured him with a sword of honour, and, what was to prove more important, he was given a commission as Lieut.-Colonel by the King.

**Bengal Trouble**

In 1756 news reached Madras from Bengal that the Nawab, Surajah Dowlah, had overrun the Company's settlements, captured Calcutta and had caused 146 Europeans to be put into a small airless room for a night, during which 123 of them died, an incident which was subsequently known as 'the Black Hole of Calcutta'.

It looked as if the whole of the Company's interests in Bengal would have to be written off. Not much help could be expected from Bombay. It all depended upon Madras.

The Board in Madras sent for Clive from Cuddalore. The serious situation was discussed, and it was decided to send the whole of the squadron under Admiral Watson and all the land forces that could be spared to Bengal. Colonel Clive was given command of the land forces. This was when his military rank saved an awkward situation. Adlercron was also a Lieut.-Colonel and was unpleasant about his own rights in the matter. If Clive had not had the rank there might have been another of those unseemly quarrels and bad decisions which from time to time set back the progress of the Company's interests.

Watson's fleet sailed with the force under Clive's command. The troops consisted of :—

600 of the 39th Foot.

300 of the Company's European Regiment (which was one day to become the 102nd Foot and then the Dublin Fusiliers).

1,500 Madras Sepoys.

On arrival Clive rapidly took Calcutta, on January 10, 1757.

Then followed a curious delay of five months, in which the Nawab vacillated. Clive's force was very small in comparison with the masses at the disposal of the Nawab. But Clive was busy.

**Plassey**

In June things looked like coming to a head. On the 21st of June Clive, with his army of 3,000, which had been increased by 600 additional arrivals, was near a river adjacent to the village of Plassey. On the other side of the river was the huge army of the Nawab, 58,000 strong. The Nawab had 40,000 infantry, 18,000 cavalry, and 50 heavy guns. Clive held a Council of War and decided to retreat. Heavy rain came on, to the great relief of some of his officers who looked upon it as the Act of Providence to ensure a safe retreat.

Clive suddenly changed his mind. On 22nd June at 6 a.m., he crossed the river Baggiruttee. By midnight he had reached the now famous Mango Tope. The battle started at daybreak on the 23rd of June. It continued until dark, by which time the whole army of the Nawab had been routed and was in flight.

Those are the actual facts.

There is something much more behind it. In the Spanish Civil War of 1936 and 1937, General Franco was not the first person to use the Fifth Column. Clive was more of an expert at it than he was. Clive spent the five months in 1757 in making all preparations for shaking the morale of the Nawab's generals. Hesitation started directly the battle began. Many of the Nawab's troops never fought at all.

The result of it all was that Clive regained control of the whole of Bengal. But it must be remembered that Clive took a very great risk. His secret negotiations might, up to the last moment, have gone completely astray. One thing he was sure of, the absolute reliability of his troops, of whom the majority were Madrassis!

At this point Clive leaves the Madras story. His great work in Bengal, his return to England, and his further term in Bengal have a wider compass. His life ended in tragedy. Retired in England, unemployed, ill in health, depressed by the constant personal attacks made upon him in Parliament and elsewhere, he took his own life on 22nd November 1774, aged 49, at a time when Britain badly needed the wisdom and ability of such a man if it could but have realised it.

The wider practical application of the demands of the people under democracy as it works in Britain today, and the power of a free press, go far to ensure that the jealousy and envy of politicians is subdued to the common good. The Clives of today are not discarded.

The northern defences of the Fort were almost completed, and much had been done on the western face when developments in Pondicherry threatened

Madras again. Clive was up in Bengal. The Company was much encouraged by his success there, but the Board in Madras knew that there was peril from the French looming up.

**Map V. 1758**

It will be noted that the old river was now almost filled in. The western moat was in a properly deep condition. The all-round aspect of defence was much better. And the town to the north no more offered a covered way of approach. Fort St. George was now commanded by a bold, experienced and resolute soldier, Stringer Lawrence. He made all possible preparations, water was contained in masonry tanks, food was stored, guns and ammunition prepared for action, and outposts manned. An important factor was that communication by sea was maintained. Out here in Madras, as in every other part of the world, the influence of sea power stands out every time.

SEPOY

The seige started in December 1758. It lasted 67 days, and was relieved by a powerful British Fleet on 16th February 1759. For 46 days the enemy had kept up a continual shell fire. The fire was always vigorously returned. The Fort inside was reduced to a sad wreck. Hardly any of the upper stories of the houses were intact. The church of St. Mary's was the only building not seriously injured, the reason being its bomb-proof construction.

**Siege**

A hero of the seige was Yusuf Khan, the Commandant of the Sepoys, whose bold stories and distractions were of the utmost service. His name should ever be remembered in the history of the Fort.

Blacktown had been ruthlessly pillaged by the French, who had also destroyed the village of Chepauk.

The Governor, Pigot, must be remembered for his resolute and determined attitude during the seige. He retired in 1763, was raised to the Peerage, and returned for his second term in 1775. His grave is a notable feature in St. Mary's Church.

One consequence of the siege, and of the leadership of Yusuf Khan was the organisation of the sepoys into regular battalions. Seven battalions each of 1,000 men were raised, with European officers and one Indian Commandant. Two of these battalions were to be stationed at Madras, one at Chingleput as the outpost of Madras, and the remaining four at Conjeevaram and Trichinopoly.

We now have a period of 23 years during which the Fort is being fully rebuilt. The result became

**Map VI. 1781**

by 1781 very much what the Fort is today. The entire area of the fort and its outworks is well over 100 acres. The interior encloses about 42 acres and measures 620 yards from North to South and 330 yards from East to West.

A low line of rising ground known as Hog Hill stood where the present Ordnance Lines and Medical College stand. The whole of this hill, estimated at 214,000 cubic yards of earth, was cut away and used for the filling in the old river and for making the glacis of the Fort. A European named Benfield was the principal contractor for the building. It involved an enormous amount of bricks and of all materials.

During this period of the building of the New Fort, there were two periods of severe fighting, though for the rest of the time there was no real settled peace.

**Eyre Coote**

From 1758 to 1760 a campaign against the French was in progress, the most notable feature of which was the battle of Wandiwash in which Eyre Coote defeated the French. The capture of Pondicherry followed in 1761.

Over on the West Coast, in the Bombay area, the Mahratta War lasted from 1774 to 1782, and it had its natural repercussions on this side.

**Hyder Ali**

In 1780 Hyder Ali, the Ruler of Mysore, descended upon the Carnatic with 80,000 men. Eyre Coote, now much older, defeated Hyder at Porto Novo and Pollilore. Hyder died in 1782, being succeeded by his son Tippoo who signed a Treaty of Peace in 1784. It lasted until 1790.

Throughout this period Eyre Coote and the other Generals in the Madras Service had to try to carry on a defensive war under a critical and unhelpful Board of Directors. A number of British regiments had been sent out to assist, but the Board of Directors looked upon them as being intended essentially for the DEFENCE of Madras, and they did not approve of any sort of OFFENCE. As long as the French or Hyder Ali kept at a distance, and if trade could continue in good measure, why worry? That was their attitude. Soldiers realised only too well that such a policy only asked for very serious and increasing trouble. The best Defence is Offence, a very old and true maxim.

As a result of the Directors' attitude, Eyre Coote's supply and transport were unorganized and sometimes almost non-existent. He gained great tactical successes and then was at his wits' end to know how to feed his men, how to pay them, and where to turn for ammunition. Added to this the lack of cavalry prevented him following up his successes and turning them into victories, and deprived him of proper intelligence.

The Board in Madras were an unpleasant lot of men, more concerned with their own dignity and being addressed in the proper way than in the success of the operations. Jealousy, envy and smallness of mind seemed more prevalent than usual. Coote himself was not easy to get on with, and probably irritated his colleagues by his bluntness, and by proving himself right and them wrong,—always a mistake in dealing with superiors.

Coote himself had first landed with the 39th Foot in 1754, and fought under Clive at Plassey. He was home from 1762 to 1770. Coming out in 1771, he resigned in 1772 and went to England again. In 1778 he came out for the third and last time. He died in Madras in 1773, and was temporarily interred in St. Mary's Church. Later, his remains were taken to England.

**Tippoo**

In the year 1790 Tippoo, son of Hyder Ali, made war against the Company's ally, the Raja of Travancore. The campaign of General Medows (whose portrait may be seen in the Banqueting Hall at Government House) in Coimbatore and Dindigul, having proved indecisive, the Governor-General, Lord Cornwallis, decided to come to Madras from Calcutta and conduct the war himself. He had previously arranged for the co-operation of the Nizam and of the Mahrattas. He arrived in Madras with reinforcements of troops and proceeded to advance straight on Bangalore, ignoring the enemy who were in force near Pondicherry. He took the Fort, in which action Lieut.-Colonel Moorhouse was killed. Moorhouse was a fine and gallant soldier. A tablet in St. Mary's relates to him.

The campaign continued up to the vicinity of Seringapatam where Tippoo accepted terms and lost half of his territory.

A statue of Lord Cornwallis was erected on the eastside of the Barrack Square. It was later moved to a position in front of the Custom House, opposite the present Harbour, where the canopy, with its columns, can still be seen. At a later date it was removed from there on account of ill-feeling caused by certain reliefs on its base. It is now at the end of the Long Room of the Connemara Library, which is worth a visit.

Ever since the Treaty of 1792 Tippo Sultan had been watching for a favourable opportunity for resuming the contest with the British. He had been in touch with the French and had had a promise of assistance from Napoleon himself.

The New Governor-General, Lord Mornington (afterwards Marquis Wellesley) decided to take the initiative and started to prepare. His brother, Lieut.-Colonel the Hon. Arthur Wellesley (afterwards the great Duke of Wellington) had arrived in 1798 with his Regiment, the 33rd Foot. His house in Fort St. George stands today almost exactly as it was then.

**Wellington**

It is probable that Col. Wellesley had some say in the transport arrangements for the coming campaign, for he later became one of the world's greatest Supply Generals. It is fitting that Wellesley House in the Fort should have been so long occupied by the Royal Indian Army Service Corps as an Officers' Mess.

Arthur Wellesley had served on the Continent in Europe before coming to India. Although very young, he was a Member of Parliament besides being a soldier. He was a great leader and brought out a considerable library with him.

He was at Calcutta first, where his brother, Lord Mornington, later to become Marquis Wellesley, was Governor-General. While there he studied the position in South India carefully, and was fully aware of troop locations and defence dispositions in the Carnatic. He could see that one thing stood out clearly when looking at reports of previous operations : lack of transport and supply.

His regimen., the 33rd Foot (now 1st Bn. Duke

of Wellington's Regt.) arrived in Madras in September 1798 after a four-week journey from Calcutta. Wellesley came too and took up proper regimental soldiering again, but he was not quite the same as an ordinary Lieut.-Colonel as he had his family connection and had deeply studied the Carnatic problem from a wide aspect.

The second Lord Clive, son of the great Robert Clive, was Governor of Madras. He was a steady rather difficult and slow sort of man, who had to be given new ideas gradually. Probably he took after his mother. Nevertheless Wellesley was successful with him and convinced him of the immediate importance of reorganising and building up a transport and supply system.

In 1799, when Wellesley was just 30 years old, the war against Tippoo Sultan was ready to begin.

**Seringapatam**

The army concentrated at Vellore. Wellesley commanded a division, consisting of his own 33rd, 6 battalions of Company's sepoys and 4 battalions of the Nizam's troops. He was still only a Colonel. General Harris was in command of the whole force, with General Baird under him.

The army, this time well-equipped and supplied, went forward fairly easy, brushed aside opposition and reached the outskirts of Seringapatam. The battle was fairly soon over. Tippo was found dead with a bullet through his head, and was given an impressive and dignified funeral.

Now came a problem, the reorganization and reconstituting of Mysore. General Baird would normally have been given the Command at Seringapatam, but he was brusque, tactless and had a prejudice against Indians. General Harris decided to put Wellesley in command. Arthur took the order himself to General Baird and showed it to him. It must have been indeed an awkward moment, but it did not seem to worry Wellesley who asked Baird please to finish his breakfast.

The whole situation in South India now changed. For the first time since 1640 the British were really in complete control. There was still trouble brew-

GUN TRANSPORT

ing further to the north-west, but in the great plains of the Carnatic peace had come, which was to last without any serious threats until the Japanese invasion appeared to be so imminent in 1942.

The story of the battle of Assaye, which now follows, does not really concern the fortunes of Fort St. George so much, but it must be mentioned since it was won mainly by Madrassi troops.

**Assaye**

After two years in Seringapatam or roundabout in Mysore, Wellesley was ordered to prepare for operations against the Mahrattas. All this time he had remained a Colonel, in spite of having the command of the troops in Mysore, Malabar and Canara. He seems to have borne the grievance well, and to have gone on doing his duty. His promotion was, as usual, affected by the constant friction regarding the relative rights of the Company's Officers as against the Regular Officers.

In December 1802 he heard of his promotion to Major-General. At last it had come after long delay.

He immediately got to work on his usual preparations. He knew that the secret of all success lay in supply—animals, forage, containers for rice, salt meat, salt, sugar, and even barrels for arrack. He installed supply points, advanced bases and worked out his line of march with great thoroughness.

He marched in February 1803 and met the Mahrattas on September 23rd at Assaye unexpectedly. It looks as if his information was still at fault, due probably to the same old trouble of not using enough cavalry.

The enemy had about 32,000 men with 100 guns, while Wellesley had not more than 6,000. This time, unlike Plassey which had been fought by Clive nearly fifty years before, the battle was furious and bitter. The Mahrattas were well trained and disciplined. They had a number of European officers and were in good positions.

The British force consisted of three British regiments, the 74th and 78th Foot and the 19th Dragoons. The whole of the rest were Madras troops, the 4th, 8th, 10th, and 24th Madras Infantry and the 4th, 5th, and 7th Madras Cavalry.

It was a complete victory. It was the first victory at which the future Duke of Wellington had commanded-in-chief. At Seringapatam he had been under Harris. The British losses were heavy—198 Europeans and 230 Sepoys killed, 442 Europeans and 696 Sepoys wounded, a total of about 1,500 out of a force of 6,000.

After this there was further fighting elsewhere as the situation was gradually cleared up. In 1805 Wellesley sailed for England, having been made a Knight of the Bath, and with a great reputation. He had much work before him.

**Peace**

From now onwards the Battle History of Fort St. George virtually ceases. Peace spread its beneficent influence all over the Carnatic. Houses grew up all along Mount Road in Madras, in Egmore and in Nungumbaukam. The City spread itself.

A long period of fifty years follows, of development, and administration, the building of roads and tanks, the evolution of a system of justice, law and order, and the expansion of agriculture which was the most vital thing of all. Trade developed, shipping increased, and except for internal troubles of no great magnitude from time to time, the Madras Army had little to do in its own territory.

It played its part in other places, Mauritius, Burma, Malacca, and China.

Perhaps the high-light of this period, of the first half of the nineteenth century, was the great

**Munro**

Governor, Sir Thomas Munro, whose statue stands on the Island just opposite the Stanley Club. He had been a young officer at the time of Eyre Coote, had served through the Mysore campaign with Wellesley, and was made Governor in 1820. He was responsible for the Ryotwari System of Land Tenure. By this system the ryot—the small holder—pays his taxes direct to Government instead of through a grasping intermediary. This is one of the reasons for the contentment and relative prosperity of the people of South India, for there are few Zemindars or big landholders in South India. The ordinary agriculturist holds his land direct from Government and has all contact direct with Government through the Collector.

The Madras Presidency is divided into 25 Districts each of which is something like a group of counties—say Yorkshire. Over each District is a Collector. It is an old name, meaning that he collects the revenue. But he is much more than that. He is, in a way, the District Governor. With him there is usually a District Judge who is over the subordinate judiciary of the District, and there is a Deputy Superintendent of Police. These men administer the country.

If we look back and think how it was all gradually worked out, the years of patient labour to build up something that was fair to everyone, built up on a foundation of justice, a system that works today, smoothly and efficiently, we must salute with admiration those men who made it all, and of them the outstanding figure is Thomas Munro.

Read the words on his tomb-stone in St. Mary's Church. He longed to go home. He had done long and faithful service. He was old. He was tired. He was persuaded to agree to an extension of his tenure of office. Duty made him agree. Away, up-country, visiting a district, that Grand Old Man fell ill and died. Like many another he never reached the happy garden in England to which he had looked forward all his service.

MADRAS INFANTRY (Officers in Full Dress)

The year 1857 saw the very grave troubles

1857 in the North of India, usually called the Indian Mutiny. Down in Madras there was no trouble, because there never was any cause for trouble. Ominous news grew into disasters. The whole north appeared to be ablaze. Not since 1756 had such a serious position been evident.

The whole Madras Army was made available by the Governor, Lord Harris, grandson of the General who was commanding at the time of Wellington. A strong force was despatched to Bengal, and it marched through Cawnpore and Lucknow and the Mutiny ended. For the third time Madras troops saved India.

At Plassey under Clive, at Assaye under Wellesley, and in the Mutiny of 1857, men from the Carnatic Plains went out to fight. They were not massive impressive warriors. They never appeared as great subjects for the author or the artist. They never advertised themselves. They were just plain

Madrassis, Naidus, Mudaliars, Naickers, Pillays, Muslims and Christians. Quiet, hardworking, intelligent, efficient, disciplined, eating the same food, with no animosity towards each other, they were the men of South India, grand stuff.

At that date 1857, the oldest Volunteer Regiment in India now existing, the Madras Guards, was raised by Lord Harris to defend the City in the absence of the Regular Army. It was not the first volunteer force to exist, as the Second Lord Clive had formed two volunteer battalions in the year 1801 when there was a severe threat from the French while the main bulk of the Madras Army was away in Mysore. Lord Clive commanded one battalion himself, while the other was under the command of the Chief Justice. As they were later disbanded there is no continuity, but there is a fair claim to a connection with the gentlemen who paraded in the early mornings with their muskets in 1801. Not far from the Fort, entering the River Cooum from the North, and leaving it to the South, runs the great Buckingham Canal. It was constructed in three main stages between 1802 and 1882 and derived its name from the Duke of Buckingham and Chandos, Governor 1875-1880, during whose time the third and main stage was executed. A portrait of the Duke may be seen in the Officers' Mess of the Madras Coast Battery, the descendant of the Madras Artillery Volunteers, 'The Duke's Own', founded by the Duke of Buckingham in 1875.

The Fort shows little change in its outward defences since its completion in 1781, but the old 'Fort

**Map VII. 1862**

Square' has gone. All that remains is the old Governor's House in the Centre (marked 'A') with its eastward link and its two arms. It is interesting to try to work out how this was incorporated in the present Secretariat buildings. The old Exchange Building (marked 'M') became the Officers' Mess of the British Infantry Regiment in the Fort in this year, 1862.

Divisions between the houses are marked, as this is the period when houses in the Fort were still private property before Government bought them up.

**Map VIII. 1939**

This is the Fort today. Most of the outer ravelins have been removed, and the lesser moat extensions filled in. The British Military Hospital in the south was presumably the cause for part of the removals and levelling. The Secretariat shows great changes, and expansion. In the West new Married Quarters replaced old buildings near to St. George's Gate. The greatest change is hardly noticeable, for it is at the bottom of the map, the retreat of the sea from the region of the East Curtain, due to the effect upon the beach made by the construction of the Harbour in 1875.

And so we have Fort St. George today.

# A WALK ROUND THE FORT

The first part of this book has told something of the people who lived in this Fort and of the things that happened.

Now follows a suggestion for an actual visit to those streets, houses and ramparts. The book may be taken for reference at each point of the tour, but as the enthusiasm of the writer may have caused him to expand unduly at times, it might be as well to read this through before setting out, instead of standing with the hot sun glaring on to the pages. And also, you may not wish your fancies to be disturbed as you go round.

**1.** Start at the Guard-Room on the South side of the Barrack Square, marked 'G' in Map VIII. Note the brass plates of some of the British Regiments that have occupied it, particularly the 39th Foot.

**2. Now walk to the Church.** Stop inside the gate. On the right you will find the oldest English gravestone probably in India, that of the wife of Aaron Baker, Governor of Madras. She died in 1652. Look at some of the other stones. Originally they were in the cemetery which was where the Law College now stands. The French used these stones as platforms for guns, and for cover in the sieges of 1746 and 1758. They were therefore afterwards removed from the cemetery and brought to St. Mary's Church. Later, when the Fort was threatened during the wars with Mysore, and when there was danger of attack by the French,

the stones were taken up on to the ramparts for use as platforms for the guns. They were not returned to their present position until 1807. Many of them were broken, unfortunately.

**3. Enter the Church.** See the thickness of the walls—4 feet. The roof is 2 feet thick of solid masonry, built to withstand French cannon-balls from the sea. This Church was designed and built in 1680 by Edward Fowle, Master-Gunner of the Fort which also meant 'Chief Engineer', as the Engineers and Gunners were all one in those days. See the brass plate above the offertory-box, to his memory. The Governor, STREYNSHAM MASTER, collected the whole of the money for building this

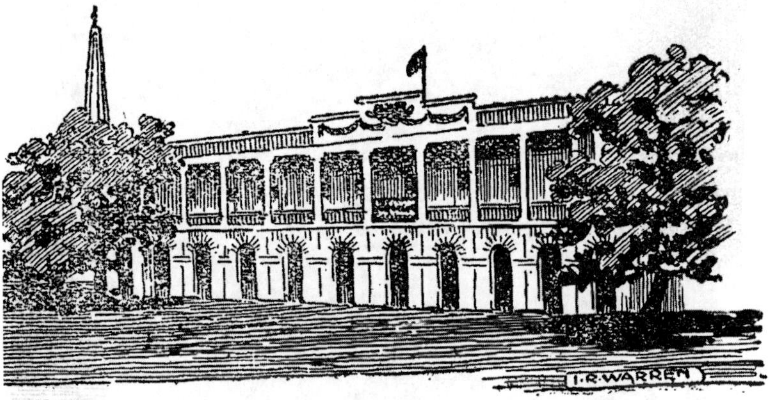

Church from private subscriptions. You will see his portrait in the Vestry.

**4. Please sign your name in the visitors' book.**

**5. Go up the centre Aisle.** Observe the memorials to the two Admirals on your right. Sir Samuel Hood and Drury. Except in the Monsoon Season, there were probably always ships lying in the Roads off the shore here. Sea-power had much influence on the history of this place as it did upon the rest of the world. Hood is buried in the centre of the aisle.

**6. Stand on the Chancel steps,** and look down at the tomb-stones. Note the four Governors

and a Commander-in-Chief, who are buried here. The most interesting is the one marked with a plain cross and the words 'In Memoriam'. In 1779 Lord Pigot was in his second term as Governor. There was great friction between him and the Commander in-Chief, Sir Robert Fletcher. Pigot seems to have decided to supersede Fletcher, but the Commander-in-Chief took action first. Pigot was driving up Mount Road in a carriage with a colonel when they were met and surrounded by a troop of cavalry. The colonel informed Pigot that he was under arrest by the order of the Commander-in-Chief. He was kept at Government House under arrest, lived comfortably and entertained his friends while the orders of the Company in London were awaited. After a few months Pigot died. He was buried in St. Mary's Church, but the exact position of the grave was lost.

A hundred years later, the Duke of Buckingham, Governor of Madras, was making alterations to the Church when an important grave was discovered. The Duke decided that it must be Pigot's. He therefore placed a stone over the grave, but owing to the doubt the simple cross and the two words were all that were inscribed.

Observe Munro, the great Governor who was responsible for the Ryotwari system of Land Tenure, which brings the actual holder of land into direct contact with the Government. Note the memorial to Munro on the wall near-by. The great statue of him, mounted on a horse, is in the centre of the Island, near the Stanley Club.

**7. Now turn round** and view the picture over the altar. No one knows where it came from. It probably was brought from Pondicherry, and was from the School of Raphael. It is a copy of his Last Supper, and may have been done in his studio. Some experts think that he is responsible for some of the centre of the picture. His studio was a successful business, and he made his pupils do much of his less important work.

**8. Where you now stand,** on these steps, Margaret Maskelyne and Robert Clive knelt to be married, for these were the original altar steps. The Church formerly ended where the roof vaulting finishes. The present sanctuary and vestry were added later.

**9. Go to the south aisle.** See the Moorhouse memorial first, because, as a work of art, it is poor, which is a pity, for Moorhouse was a very gallant soldier

**10. Now go east** to the next tablet, and look at the Barry Close memorial, a glorious work by the great sculptor, Flaxman, many of whose productions are in St. Paul's in London, and Westminster Abbey. Observe the perfect muscles, sinews, and the folds of every garment, and the amazing reality which might almost come to life. The British Soldier and the Sepoy stand enclosing the Hindu (just like the Brahmin of today) and the Mohammedan. Inspect it closely.

**11.** If the vestry is open, **Go in and see the portraits there.**

**12. Move across to the arch near to the pulpit.** The colours, the copper plate, and the tablet below may well be called the tragedy of the Dublin Fusiliers.

They were raised in Madras as the First battalion of the European Regiment of the East India Company, and consisted of men recruited in

London, and brought out to Madras, together with a certain number of Portuguese and Anglo-Indians, and at one time of Swiss and Germans. They became the Royal Madras Fusiliers, and were later taken over by the British Government. They then became the 102nd Foot, to be later named the Royal Dublin Fusiliers.

Founded in Madras in 1668, they had a long and glorious battle record, as the honours on the plate show.

In 1922 they were again serving in Madras, the city of their origin, when Southern Ireland became an independent republic, and the tragic order was given for the disbandment of this regiment.

**13.** See the statue of Conway, the Soldiers' Friend. A tradition says that he was responsible for the proviso to Section 138 of the Army Act, by which a soldier must actually receive a minimum of one penny a day in spite of all deductions and penalties. In the old days soldiers had so many deductions that they often went for months with no pay at all. A tradition here says that Conway improved the accommodation in King's Barracks.

**14. Move to the north aisle.** We now come to the most famous of all the memorials in this Church, the Schwartz memorial. The Court of Directors of the Honourable East India Company were hard-fisted business-men, but they went to the trouble and expense of getting this done by the leading sculptor of the day, Bacon, and sending it on the long journey by sailing ship, to be landed by boats on this beach and then erected here—all for a missionary.

Read the amazing tribute of Hyder Ali, 'Let him pass, for he is a holy man'. Schwartz was one of the outstanding figures of the eighteenth century.

**15. Move to the next memorial.** Here is a Flaxman again. You will notice the same models for the Brahmin and for the Muslim. On the right is the Company's servant, probably a Member of Council. Note his clothes. The I.C.S. wear the same with very little change, as their full-dress uniform today. Outside on the right is the Army Officer. Note the interesting details of his uniform, particularly about his collar.

**16.** Below is the sad tablet to the last of the Madras Regiments on disbandment. Remember that they took a great part in the victories of Plassey, Seringapatam, Assaye, and in quelling the 1857 Mutiny. The same men are in the Madras Sappers and Miners, which has always been, and remained, a 'Corps d'élite', and was not disbanded. Somehow the military reputation of Madras fell away. The Presidency was far from the Frontier, the traditional training ground of the Indian Army. Retrenchment forced reductions and the Madras regiments went.

The war of 1939 saw a speedy revival of Madras recruitment, which, by the beginning of 1945 had produced the remarkable result of 22 per cent of the Indian Army being from the Madras Presidency.

**17. Go towards the South Door.** See the gallery under the tower, where the Governor and Council sat in their wigs and glory, with their wives, while servants fanned them from behind. Note the beautifully carved Carolean heads just below the hand-rail. The varnish is a pity. Successive organs were at different times in the gallery, probably at the back.

Below is a beautiful old altar-cloth, in a case. It cannot be used now because of age. It is probably of Continental origin.

Note the tablet to Burgoyne. He was not the Burgoyne of Saratoga fame, but a relative of his. Also see the font, where Yale's children were baptized.

TOWER OF ST. MARY'S CHURCH

**18. Go out of the South Door** of the Church, across the garden, and into the room opposite to see the model of the Fort. Its exact date is not known, but it is certainly after 1820 and before 1862. Presumably reasons of security prevented models of the guns being put into position. This is a pity as there was a fine armament round the walls. One is apt to forget today the number of artillerymen who must have lived near their pieces. When the ordnance became obsolete, a number of them were too heavy to be economically taken away and therefore they were sunk in parts of the moat. In front of the flagstaff, in 1942, when the moat was being urgently deepened to make a supply of water available for the A.R.P. Service of the Secretariat, a fine large piece was exposed. It appeared to be one of the early rifled muzzle-loading guns of about nine inch calibre. (See illustration.)

One of the 4.7 inch guns used against the German Cruiser 'Emden' in 1914 was eventually given its last resting place in the moat on the western side. Some day antiquarians may make interesting discoveries in the moats.

A fine 18-pdr. cannon of the 1800 period stood just north of the Secretariat for a long time. It is now in the Naval Barracks.

**19. Leave the Model Room and go into the street on its eastern side.** Here we are in St. Thomas' Street, (marked 'T' in Map VIII) long known by its derisive or envious name of 'Snobs' Alley'. Here the senior men lived. Colonels and majors of the British regiments occupied these quarters. Before that the Company's Members of Council had houses. The lower parts of the houses may date from before the sieges of 1746 and 1758, but it is known that in those sieges the upper parts of almost all the houses in the Fort were badly damaged. The upper parts probably date from the rebuilding period of 1760 to 1780.

Various houses have been pointed out as 'where Clive tried to commit suicide'. It is definitely NOT known where Clive lived as a young man. If we think about it sensibly it is clear that there must have been someone in the Fort corresponding to the Station Staff Officer or Fort Accommodation Officer who allocated quarters. Robert Clive himself was Fort Steward at one time, which may have included these duties. Conditions have not varied much. There is always a scramble for quarters. Therefore Clive, like all who have followed him for two hundred years, probably lived in all the quarters at some time or other, being turned out and shifted according to seniority, or because he was, or was not noisy, or for some other reason.

Look down the street. Think of the circumstances of daily life in those times. Everyone was occupied in private trading, besides his own duties. There is a remarkable amount of storage room in the gound floor of each house. They were obviously not living rooms. Try to picture bales of cotton prints and chintzes ready for export, cases of English fancy articles ready for disposal to Indian merchants, barrels of wine, boxes of all sizes, planks of wood being carefully collected for future use, possibly cases of indigo, sacks of rice, or of spices, and even furniture or musical instruments for future sale. Down or up the street these were carried. Bullock bandies blocked the roads in spite of all sorts of orders about traffic. Ladies going out in their palanquins looked furiously at the obstructions, at the same time looking with interest at what was coming out of the house next door. Horses stood by their grooms, servants pushed past each other. Indeed the scene must have been animated. In the eighteenth century a young married couple had to have a minimum of thirty servants.

Perhaps a more peaceful touch might come from the balcony down the street where the light caught the fair ringlets of a young lady sitting in a long chair waiting hopefully for the sea breeze.

There in the first floors of these houses the men and their wives lived, brought up their children, dined, wined and died. Mortality was great. Fifty per cent of newly arrived soldiers died during their first three years.

**20.** Immediately on the right, just next down the street from the model room, is a big warehouse, with its high roof supported by pillars. You will probably find it closed, for it still contains stores. One can picture two young writers, only a year or two out from England, clad in loose tussore silk garments which they wore on informal occasions. (and on other occasions when their seniors could not see them).

One says to the other 'Do you feel the better for your adventure on the road from Chingle-put?'

'Adventure?' replies the other. 'I escaped but with the skin of my teeth. I am blamed for losing the merchandise of the Company when there is not sufficient guard to keep off a few stray bandicoots, much less the horsemen of Mysore. It is indeed time that we made full and proper conquest of this country.'

'Count the cost. Sum up the pagodas that it would mean. Indeed the dividends in London would look sorry.'

'Dividends? That is indeed all that our Most Honourable Court in London can think of.'

'And why not? Give me wealth, say I, and may it be soon.'

'Is that the only reason that we are here?'

'What other?'

'It may be that we have a duty to this country and to its people, to give them good government

SNOBS' ALLEY—1760

and peace. It behoves us surely to consider how best that can be done.'

' By conquering, by battalions, by generals and armies. The devil take you for a dreamer. Our Right Honourable Masters want but one thing, trade. Neither they, nor our masters here will care to hear your sentiments. Come with me to the Tavern and taste Master Yardley's new madeira.'

So they go off together as many young men have since, wondering why they are so far from home and what it is all for.

**21. The first house on the left,** looks old, but the first two bays are comparatively new, as will be seen in comparison with the model. This has been for many years the residence of the senior officer in the Fort. Subsequently it became a Headquarters' Mess, and then accommodated Nursing Sisters. The southern part of it probably dates from 1770. There is nothing of particular interest inside it.

**22. Stop at the last house on the left,** look inside and see the fine carved staircase which goes up to the second storey. It might well be in any building in the Middle Temple in London. This is one of the oldest houses in the Fort, in all probability.

**23. Post office.** Immediately to the south is a small vacant plot of uneven ground where a house was demolished at one time. The Post Office was moved there after the ' Fort Square ' (where the Secretariat now is—not the Barrack Square) was pulled down.

**24. Stop at the last house on the right.** This is the Chaplain's house. Your guide will take you into a room to see the Silver Plate and

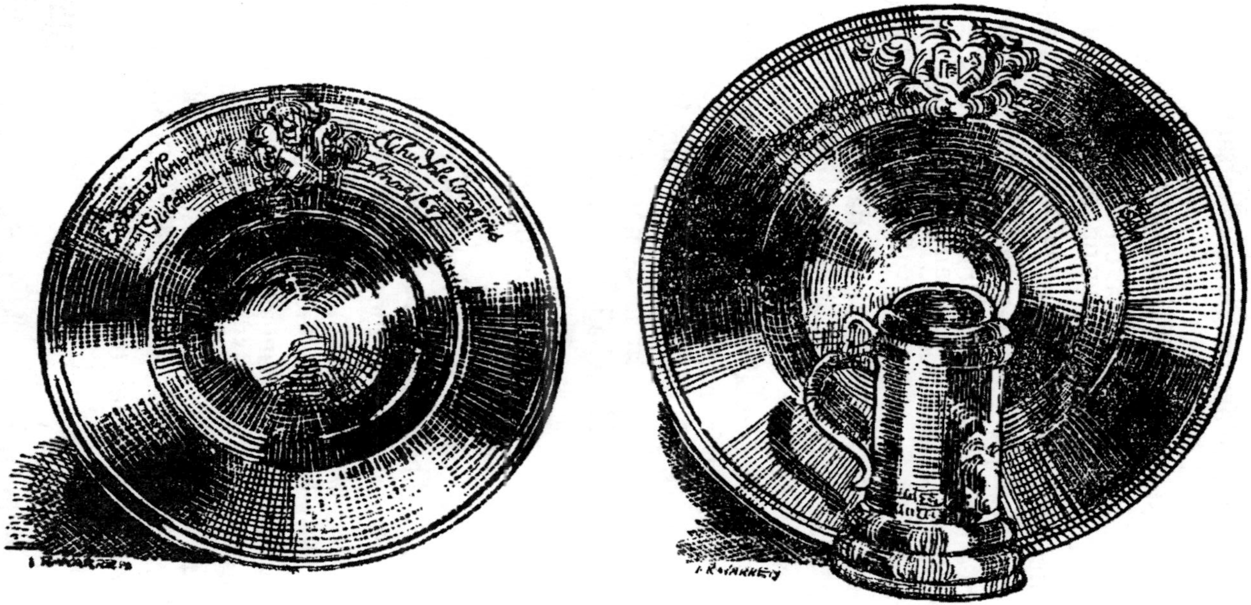

YALE GOLDSBOROUGH PLATE

the Records. These are the most important treasures in the Fort.

(i) The Yale Plate. See page 57.

(ii) The Goldsborough Flagon and Basin. See page 57.

(iii) The fine Danish plate and vessels which came from Tranquebar when the Danes sold their settlement to the East India Company in 1845. See the Danish monogram, D.O.C. on the large alms dish, and the ebony stick with silver bands for handling round the alms offerings bag, dated 1687. Note the plain little silver gilt paten and the silver gilt chalice dated 1689.

(iv) The Sacramental Plate of Pulicat Church which were probably handed over when the Dutch possessions were all taken over by the British in 1824. The square paten is of a simple and very beautiful design. The chalice is unusual and most interesting.

Nearly all the above are European work of the 17th century.

(v) Observe next Streynsham Master's Bible, dated 1660. The first three pages are photostat copies from the volume in the British Museum. The remainder is original. It was presented to the church in 1881 by Mr. C. G. Master, of the Madras Civil Service, a descendant of the former Governor.

(vi) See the old key of the church which was in use for 140 years. Note it because in another part of the room you will see a much more diverting key.

(vii) On the wall see the plan of the Church and the original Minister's Lodgings which were at the western end of the Church.

(viii) The magnificent old registers are under a glass cover, for inspection. They date from the founding of the church in 1680 up to the present day, with a gap of three years from 1746 when the French were in occupation. Note the entry of Clive's marriage in one, and Arthur Wellesley's signature as a witness to a wedding in the other.

(ix) In the centre of the room is a fine old chest of great capacity. It offers one solution to the old mystery tale of the 'Mistletoe Bough'. If the bride had hid in that chest and let the lid close on her, you will note how the clasps fall down and make any attempts to open from the inside impossible. Sounds from inside would be unlikely to be heard.

(x) Try the key in the old safe in the corner. It works perfectly. Take it out and observe its intricate construction. Indeed a collector's treasure.

(xi) Lastly read the Company's prayer in the frame on the wall.

**25. Observe the spacious storerooms** on the ground floor, as in all the houses in this street. Until recently there was a deep brick bath in one of these rooms, but it was cleared away unobserved by authority, during renovations.

**26. Go outside the house, turn right and up the slope on to the ramparts** (marked 'R' in Map VIII).

This gives you an idea of the massiveness of the fortification. The sea originally came up to the road which you see below you as you look eastwards. You can imagine the rollers breaking on to the sandy beach just where the road now runs. The spray often came into the houses facing the ramparts, during the monsoon. The Harbour in 1875 caused the great accretion of sand that now forms

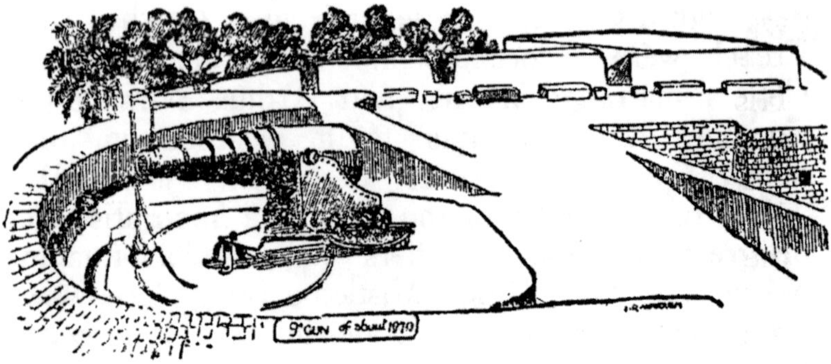

San Thome Bastion

the wide foreshore, due to the current, which for nine months in the year runs from South to North.

Underneath you, and all round the ramparts of the Fort are vaulted chambers, used as stores for ammunition and arms, and also for living quarters for the troops. There was no proper barrack accommodation during the first hundred years of the Fort's life. Soldiers lived where they could or were billeted. Later there were barracks of sorts. King's Barracks will be seen later.

**27. Walk along the ramparts to the west.** Below you on the left, the British Military Hospital has replaced the old outer defences. Note the ventilators from the vaults below, and the emplacements for cannon.

**28. Note Wellesley House** of which you get an excellent view as you pass over the San Thome Gate. Wellesley had a large library, and, doubtless you could see his books from where you stand looking across the balustrade and into his drawing room. The house is unaltered since his residence there, but there is no feature of particular interest inside. For many years it has been the residence and Mess of the R.I.A.S.C., which is very fitting as Wellington was one of the greatest of supply generals.

Presumably it looked very much as it does now His book-shelves would be visible from where you stand looking into his large drawing-room.

**29. Wallajah Bastion** (marked 'J' in Map VIII). This great bastion comes as a surprise, for the ordinary passer-by in the Fort would not imagine the existence of such a large elevated place which in peace contained two tennis courts. Proceed across it and climb on to the parapet. This gives a clear view of the strength of the Western defences. Observe the loopholes low down in the brick wall of the moat opposite. A tunnel runs along all the way behind the loopholes, linking them up Sharpshooters were placed there when an attack was imminent to shoot down any enemy who got so close to the walls that they could not be fired at from above.

SOUTH CURTAIN

Note also the wide field of fire afforded by the carefully graded slope of the glacis.

**30. Walk back** to the nearest ramp and descend it. It has been well worn by the wheels of many a piece of ordnance.

**31. Take the narrow road** ahead and look into one of the vaults under the ramparts.

**32. At Wellesley House** turn to the left, reading the inscription on the tablet.

**33. Pass the pile of Cannon Balls and Shells** at the entrance of the former Arsenal. The studded shells are interesting and may have been used in a gun similar to the one lying in the moat, mentioned on page 52. (See illustration.)

**34. Clive's House** (marked 'C' in Map VIII) bears a tablet whose inscription is of beautiful simplicity :—

'ROBERT 1ST LORD CLIVE
LIVED IN THIS BUILDING
IN THE YEAR 1753
TRULY GREAT IN ARMS
AND
IN COUNCIL
HE FOUNDED AN EMPIRE.'

He probably only lived here for a year. It was afterwards known as 'Admiralty House'. The second Lord Clive used it later as his residence.

**35. Pass across the barrack square and into King's Barracks** (marked 'K' in Map VIII). Here the British Battalion stationed at Madras has had its quarters for nearly two centuries. The Barracks were built in 1755 and 1756 and were extended in 1762. They were called 'Kings' Barracks,' because they 'lodged the King's Regiment ever since they have been at the Presidency', according to a report made in 1756. The regiment mentioned was the 39th Foot.

**36. Go north along Choultry Gate Street** to the Garrison Theatre (marked 'T' in Map VIII). Though the excellent stage is of modern construction made by a Bomb Disposal Company in 1944, the dressing-rooms, enclosed in massive walls, are part of a very old building dating from about 1740.

**37. Walk past Middle Gate Street** and down Gloucester Street which contains many houses of interest.

**38. Enter the British Infantry Officers' Mess** (marked 'M' in Map VIII). This building was formerly the EXCHANGE. It was built by a number of Free Merchants between 1787 and 1790. The Northern part of the Fort, in those days, was almost entirely occupied by private houses owned by Free Merchants and others, while the Southern part consisted of the Company's residences, offices and godowns.

It is interesting to note here how 'Free Merchants' had come into being.

The Company had an absolute monopoly of trade by its first charter. During its first century it tried to prevent any one else coming in, but the entry of private English traders became inevitable in three successive stages:

1. The Company's Servants engaged in private trade as part of their perquisities.
2. Ships' Captains carried extra goods which soon developed into trade as a captains' side-line.
3. Private individuals roamed about between the English, French, Dutch and Danes,

and also travelled to Persia, Malaya, Sumatra, Java, and China, as well as into the interior of India, often being of help to the Company, but getting well established unofficially in business of their own, or in partnership with servants of the Company.

The Company tried to suppress the 'Interlopers,' as the private traders were called. Indeed they prepared to take violent action against Thomas Pitt in 1679, but he got his own back very successfully, and was taken into the Company's service, becoming Governor of Madras and grandfather of the Earl of Chatham and great-grandfather of the famous Prime-Minister, William Pitt of Napoleonic times.

Finally private traders had to be acknowledged and permitted, and were known as 'Free Merchants.'

By 1710 there were 29 European Free Merchants among the inhabitants of Madras. At that date, when Governor Pitt retired to England, there were sometimes 50 ships lying at one time in the roads at anchor off the Fort. The intensity and confusion of business, and the bustling crowded scene, can be imagined.

On this spot, where the Officers' Mess stands today, there formerly stood a house belonging to a certain Free Merchant, one Robert Hughes. His house, having been acquired, was pulled down, and this massive building went up in its place. It was made to contain Warehouses and Offices on the ground-floor, which were bomb-proof against cannon from the sea, a public Coffee Tavern, a Brokers' Office, a Committee-Room for the Managers, a Bank, and the great 'Long Room' upstairs.

Downstairs, on the Northern side of the entrance, see the room which almost certainly was the Bank, known at different times as the ' Government Bank ' and ' The Madras Bank ', which is the ancestor of the Bank of Madras, which later fused with the Bombay and Bengal Banks to form The Imperial Bank of India whose great building stands in First Line Beach today.

Go up the fine old staircase to the Long Room. This forms today the dining-room, ante-room and billiard-room of the Mess. During the Exchange days, early in the nineteenth century, this room was filled with ships' captains and their officers, merchants and their clerks, brokers, dubashes, and numerous employees engaged in ' exposing merchandise for sale by sample '. The great gallery may have been filled with clerks at their tables, taking down details of transactions called up from below. The adjoining room with its wooden pillared gallery round three sides may have served a similar purpose.

The Long Room, besides being the Exchange, was used for public meetings and entertainments. Four large portraits hung on its panels, Sir Eyre Coote, General Medows, Lord Cornwallis and Marquis Wellesley. These are now in the Banqueting Hall.

In the Committee Room disputes were settled and arbitrations conducted, so that in many ways this fulfilled the functions of a Chamber of Commerce.

At other times the Governor entertained here, though he also entertained in the large room in Clive's House (Admiralty House) until the Banqueting Hall of Government House was built in 1805. (Note that the Banqueting Hall should certainly be visited to complete this story by seeing the portraits there.)

The rooms on the ground floor were used at times as auction rooms and as a subscription library.

In 1826 the Government rented the building for its own public offices. In 1861 it became the Officers' Mess of the British Regiment quartered in the Fort.

MADRAS INFANTRY (32nd Regt.) A.D. 1845

It was not until 1882 that the Government bought out the shareholders and ceased paying rent.

There were, of course, other Officers' Messes in the Fort, of the Company's European Regiment founded in 1668, of the 39th Foot which arrived in 1754, and of all the subsequent regiments. Possibly the 15th and 16th Hanoverians who were in Madras at the time of Eyre Coote had their Messes somewhere in the Fort. There were many camps spread around Madras. St. Thomas Mount was an early cantonment, and so were Pallavaram and Poonamallee.

Since 1862, every second or third year a new British Battalion arrived in Madras to be stationed in the Fort, so that many British Regiments now have memories of the Officers' Mess, the great room with its fine wooden floor, where many a dinner has been held and many light feet have danced.

Wellington was often in this room, but Clive was not, since he had retired to England before it was built.

Before leaving, go out on to the spacious veranda, facing the sea, one of the coolest places in Madras. Until the Harbour was built in 1875, the sea was only twenty or thirty yards away.

The Regiment in residence will doubtless be glad to show the visitor the regimental portraits and pictures now on the walls.

Before you leave, as you stand leaning against the curved wooden railing of the small semi-circular ledge of one of the windows of the ante-room, take a look at the flagstaff on the old 'V'-shaped ramparts which project towards the sea. A wild legend is current among the present troops occupying the Fort that a ship was blown up the beach in a great storm, and had one mast remaining upright. The mast was used temporarily for signals, and was so useful that it was left there and was built over, and, to-day, under the masonry, the old ship sleeps in her solid foundation. Needless to say, there is no foundation for this charming tale.

There is however foundation for a story about

something very near that spot. In the wall below the flagstaff may be seen one of the two old sea-gates, which were bricked up in 1942 when invasion by the Japanese was a real possibility.

For many years their iron-studded doors had been closed and out of use. They were originally used for all access from the beach and from ships, all goods landed at Madras coming through them to the Customs.

When the road was laid in front of the Fort, it was felt that something should be done about the narrow little arches, that they should be enlarged or that new wide entrances should be made elsewhere to admit carriages in comfort, so that the Secretariat could be approached from the front instead of by the long detour through the Fort. Lengthy and wordy arguments took place, and at last a decision was reached to build the present approaches, with their large ornate iron work.

The doughty old warrior, who was Commander-in-Chief of Madras at the time had strenuously opposed any alteration using every argument about security and defence, but he was over-ruled. He got in the last word, however, which he later incorporated in a minute on the subject :

'Let us always remember,' he said, 'that far greater men have gone through the old gates than will ever come through the new.'

Sad old man. He had forgotten that the greatest men of the Fort's history were youths whose new and bold ideas gave them their success. The Fort is old and venerable, but the men who built it were young. Every good day is the day of young men. And there is always the individual exception whose youth of mind is the more remarkable.

# COMPARATIVE TABLE OF WORLD HISTORY AND MADRAS EVENTS

| YEAR | BRITISH AND WORLD EVENTS | KINGS OF ENGLAND | MADRAS HISTORY |
|---|---|---|---|
| A.D. 60 | Romans in occupation of Britain... | | St. Thomas martyred at St. Thomas' Mount. |
| 900 | The Cakes ... ... | ALFRED | Strong Arab tradition about St. Thomas. San Thome known in Arabic as Betumah, 'Town of Thomas'. |
| 1485 | Printing just started ... | HENRY VII. | ... |
| 1487 | Bartholomew Diaz sailed round Cape of Good Hope ... | „ | ... |
| 1492 | Columbus discovered America ... | „ | ... |
| 1497 | Cabot of Bristol discovered Newfoundland ... | „ | ... |
| 1498 | ... ... | „ | Vasco da Gama reached India by sea. Landed at Calicut. |
| 1500 | Portuguese discovered Brazil ... | „ | ... |
| 1509 | ... | HENRY VIII. | ... |
| 1521 | Martin Luther ... | „ | ... |

| YEAR | BRITISH AND WORLD EVENTS | KINGS OF ENGLAND | MADRAS HISTORY |
|---|---|---|---|
| 1522 | ... ... | HENRY VIII. | Portuguese take San Thome. |
| 1526 | Tyndale's New Testament ... | " | Baber, Moghul, Delhi. |
| 1547 | ... ... | EDWARD VI. | St. Francis Xavier at Goa. |
| 1553 | ... ... | MARY I. | ... |
| 1558 | ... ... | ELIZABETH. | ... |
| 1577 | Drake's voyage round the World. | " | ... |
| 1580 | ... ... | " | Akbar, greatest Moghul. |
| 1588 | Spanish Armada ... | " | ... |
| 1591 | Shakespeare ... | " | ... |
| 1600 | ... ... | " | East India Company founded in London. |
| 1603 | ... ... | JAMES I. | ... |
| 1605 | Gunpowder Plot ... | " | ... |
| 1609 | Colonisation of Virginia ... | " | ... |
| 1611 | Scots colonised Ulster ... | " | ... |
| 1612 | ... ... | " | East India Company at Surat. |
| 1616 | Harvey discovered circulation of the blood ... ... | " | East India Company at Masulipatam. |
| 1620 | Mayflower ... ... | " | ... |
| 1625 | ... ... | CHARLES I. | ... |
| 1626 | ... ... | " | East India Company at Armagon. |

| | | | | |
|---|---|---|---|---|
| 1637 | John Hampden | ... | ,, | ... |
| 1640 | ... | ... | ,, | Francis Day landed at Madras and built first Fort. |
| 1649 | ... | ... | CROMWELL. | ... |
| 1655 | Capture of Jamaica | ... | ,, | ... |
| 1657 | ... | ... | ,, | Siege of Fort by Mir Jumla. British defeat Moghuls at Battle of Vepery. |
| 1660 | ... | ... | CHARLES II | ... |
| 1662 | ... | ... | ,, | Acquisition of Bombay. |
| 1666 | Great Fire of London | ... | ,, | ... |
| 1672 | ... | ... | ,, | French take San Thome. |
| 1675 | ... | ... | ,, | British take San Thome. |
| 1680 | ... | ... | ,, | Fort Church built. |
| 1685 | ... | | JAMES II. | ... |
| 1687 | ... | ... | ,, | Governor Elihu Yale. |
| 1688 | Trial of the Seven Bishops | ... | WILLIAM AND MARY. | ... |
| 1690 | ... | ... | ,, | Madras attacked by the French Fleet. |
| 1700 | ... | ... | ,, | Siege of Fort by Nawab. |
| 1702 | ... | ... | ANNE. | ... |
| 1704 | Blenheim—Marlborough | ... | ,, | ... |
| 1707 | ... | | | Aurangzebe died. Collapse of Moghul Empire. |

| YEAR | BRITISH AND WORLD EVENTS | KINGS OF ENGLAND | MADRAS HISTORY |
|---|---|---|---|
| 1711 | ... ... | ANNE | S.P.C.K. Press, now Diocesan Press, founded. |
| 1714 | ... ... | GEORGE I. | ... |
| 1719 | 'Robinson Crusoe' written ... | ,, | ... |
| 1725 | Clive born at Market Drayton ... | ,, | ... |
| 1726 | ... ... | ,, | Marmalong Bridge built. |
| 1727 | ... ... | GEORGE II. | ... |
| 1730 | Wesley started preaching ... | ,, | ... |
| 1732 | Townshend of Norfolk—Turnips. | ,, | ... |
| 1741 | ... ... | ,, | New Star Pagodas minted. |
| 1743 | ... ... | ,, | Clive arrives in Madras aged 18. |
| 1745 | Prince Charlie ... ... | ,, | ... |
| 1746 | Culloden ... ... | ,, | Clive gets commission, goes to Trichinopoly. Madras captured by French. |
| 1748 | Treaty of Aix la Chapelle ... | ,, | ... |
| 1749 | ... ... | ,, | Madras returned to the British. |
| 1751 | ... ... | ,, | Clive captured Arcot aged 26. |
| 1753 | ... ... | ,, | Clive married Margaret Maskelyne. Present Fort rebuilding started. |

| | | | | |
|---|---|---|---|---|
| 1755 | ... | ... | ,, | Clive, Lieut.-Governor of Cuddalore, aged 30. |
| 1756 | ... | ... | ,, | Black Hole of Calcutta. |
| 1757 | ... | ... | ,, | Clive aged 32 with 900 English and 1,500 Sepoys to Calcutta. |
| 1758 | ... | ... | ,, | Plassey—Clive aged 33. Madras defended by Major Stringer Lawrence besieged by French under Lally for 2 months. |
| 1759 | Capture of Quebec. | ... | ,, | ... |
| 1760 | ... | ... | GEORGE III. | W a n d i w a s h—Col. Eyre Coote. |
| 1763 | ... | ... | ,, | Lord Clive Governor of Bengal. |
| 1764 | Hargreaves' Spinning Jenny | ... | ,, | ... |
| 1765 | Capt. Cook, Australia | ... | ,, | ... |
| 1767 | ... | ... | ,, | Hyder Ali attacked Madras. |
| 1768 | ... | ... | ,, | Chepauk Palace built for Nawab. |
| 1769 | ... | ... | ,, | Second raid on Madras by Hyder Ali. Blacktown Walls built. Warren Hastings Member of Council. |
| 1772 | ... | ... | ,, | Armenian Church built. |
| 1773 | Boston Tea-Party | ... | ,, | ... |

| YEAR | BRITISH AND WORLD EVENTS | KINGS OF ENGLAND | MADRAS HISTORY |
|---|---|---|---|
| 1775 | ... ... | GEORGE III. | St. Mary's Cathedral, George Town. |
| 1776 | American Independence ... | ,, | ... |
| 1779 | ... ... | ,, | Death of Governor Lord Pigot after wrongful arrest by the Commander-in-Chief General Fletcher. |
| 1781 | ... ... | ,, | Gen. Sir Eyre Coote defeated Hyder Ali at Conjeevaram. |
| 1783 | Treaty of Versailles. Peace with French. ... ... | ,, | ... |
| 1789 | French Revolution .. | ,, | ... |
| 1798 | Nile ... ... | ,, | ... |
| 1799 | ... | ,, | Col. Wellesley aged 29 took part in defeat of Tippoo at Seringapatam |
| 1800 | British capture Malta ... | ,, | ... |
| 1801 | Copenhagen ... | ,, | ... |
| 1802 | ... ... | ,, | Banqueting Hall built. |
| 1803 | ... | ,, | Mahratta War, Assaye. |
| 1805 | Trafalgar ... | ,, | Wellesley left India aged 36. |
| 1806 | Capture of Cape of Good Hope ... | ,, | Vellore Mutiny suppressed by Col. Gillespie. |

| | | | |
|---|---|---|---|
| 1809 | ... | ,, | Threatened White Mutiny—Pay. |
| 1811 | Conquest of Java ... | ,, | ... |
| 1812 | Wellington in Spain ... | ,, | ... |
| 1814 | ... ... | ,, | St. George's Cathedral built. |
| 1815 | Waterloo ... ... | ,, | War with Nepal, Lasting peace. |
| 1818 | ... ... | ,, | St. Andrew's Kirk built. |
| 1820 | ... ... | GEORGE IV. | Sir Thomas Munro. |
| 1821 | Independence of Greece ... | ,, | ... |
| 1825 | Stockton-Darlington Railway ... | ,, | ... |
| 1829 | Catholic Emancipation ... | ,, | ... |
| 1830 | ... ... | WILLIAM IV. | ... |
| 1832 | Reform Bill ... | ,, | Madras Club. |
| 1833 | Emancipation of Slaves, Factory Act, Telegraph invented ... | ,, | ... |
| 1837 | ... ... | VICTORIA. | ... |
| 1838 | ... ... | ,, | First Afghan War. |
| 1840 | Canadian Act of Union ... | ,, | ... |
| 1842 | ... ... | ,, | New Lighthouse built. |
| 1846 | Repeal of Corn Laws ... | ,, | ... |
| 1849 | ... ... | ,, | Annexation of Punjab. |
| 1851 | Discovery of gold in Australia ... | ,, | ... |
| 1852 | ... | ,, | Second Burma War—British capture Rangoon. |
| 1854 | Crimean War ... ... | ,, | Lord Harris Governor. Abolition of Nawab. |

| YEAR | BRITISH AND WORLD EVENTS | KINGS OF ENGLAND | MADRAS HISTORY |
|---|---|---|---|
| 1856 | ... | ˈICTORIA | Madras Arcot Railway built. |
| 1857 | ... | „ | Indian Mutiny—Madras Guards founded. |
| 1861 | American Civil War—Admission of Jews to Parliament ... | „ | ... |
| 1862 | Merrimac and Monitor, first iron-clads, fought ... ... | „ | Screw Pile Pier built. |
| 1866 | Great Eastern Atlantic Cable laid ... ... | „ | ... |
| 1869 | Suez Canal opened ... | „ | ... |
| 1872 | ... ... | „ | Red Hills Water Supply. |
| 1875 | ... ... | „ | Buckingham Canal, final stage. |
| 1876 | Bell invented telephone ... | „ | ... |
| 1877 | Victoria became Empress of India. | „ | Madras Harbour started. |
| 1885 | Death of Gordon in Sudan. Discovery of gold in Transvaal. Third Burma War ... | „ | ... |
| 1890 | Opening of Forth Bridge ... | „ | ... |
| 1891 | Free Education in England—Board Schools ... ... | „ | ... |
| 1894 | Manchester Ship Canal ... | „ | ... |
| 1895 | ... ... | „ | First Tramway in Madras. |

| | | | |
|---|---|---|---|
| 1898 | Omdurmam ... | ,, | ... |
| 1899 | South African War ... | ,, | ... |
| 1901 | Wireless discovered ... | EDWARD VII. | ... |
| 1904 | Russo-Japanese War ... | ,, | ... |
| 1906 | Cinemas started ... | ,, | ... |
| 1907 | ... | ,, | Madras Electric Supply started. |
| 1909 | Bleriot flew English Channel. Union of South Africa ... | ,, | ... |
| 1910 | ... | GEORGE V | ... |
| 1911 | National Insurance ... | ,, | ... |
| 1912 | Titanic sunk. Balkan War ... | ,, | ... |
| 1914 | First World War ... | ,, | Emden shelled Madras. |
| 1915 | Chemical Warfare began ... | ,, | ... |
| 1916 | Tanks first used ... | ,, | ... |
| 1918 | First World War ended ... | ,, | ... |
| 1919 | ... | ,, | Montagu-Chelmsford Reforms |
| 1924 | Ramsay Macdonald first Labour Prime Minister ... | ,, | ... |
| 1926 | Great Strike in England ... | ,, | ... |
| 1927 | Talkies started ... | ,, | ... |
| 1931 | Statute of Westminster ... | ,, | ... |
| 1933 | Trade depression ... | ,, | ... |
| 1934 | Hitler became Fuehrer of Germany ... | ,, | ... |
| 1935 | Italy invaded Abyssinia ... | ,, | ... |

| YEAR | BRITISH AND WORLD EVENTS | KINGS OF ENGLAND | MADRAS HISTORY |
|---|---|---|---|
| 1936 | Spanish Civil War began ... | EDWARD VIII. GEORGE VI. | ... |
| 1937 | Neville Chamberlain Prime Minister. Japan invading China ... | ,, | Rajagopalachariar Prime Minister of Madras. |
| 1938 | Munich ... | ,, | ... |
| 1939 | Second World War ... | ,, | ... |
| 1940 | Italy entered War ... | ,, | Sir Arthur Hope, Governor of Madras. |
| 1941 | Japan declared war on U.S.A ... | ,, | ... |
| 1942 | ... | ,, | Japanese threat to Madras. |

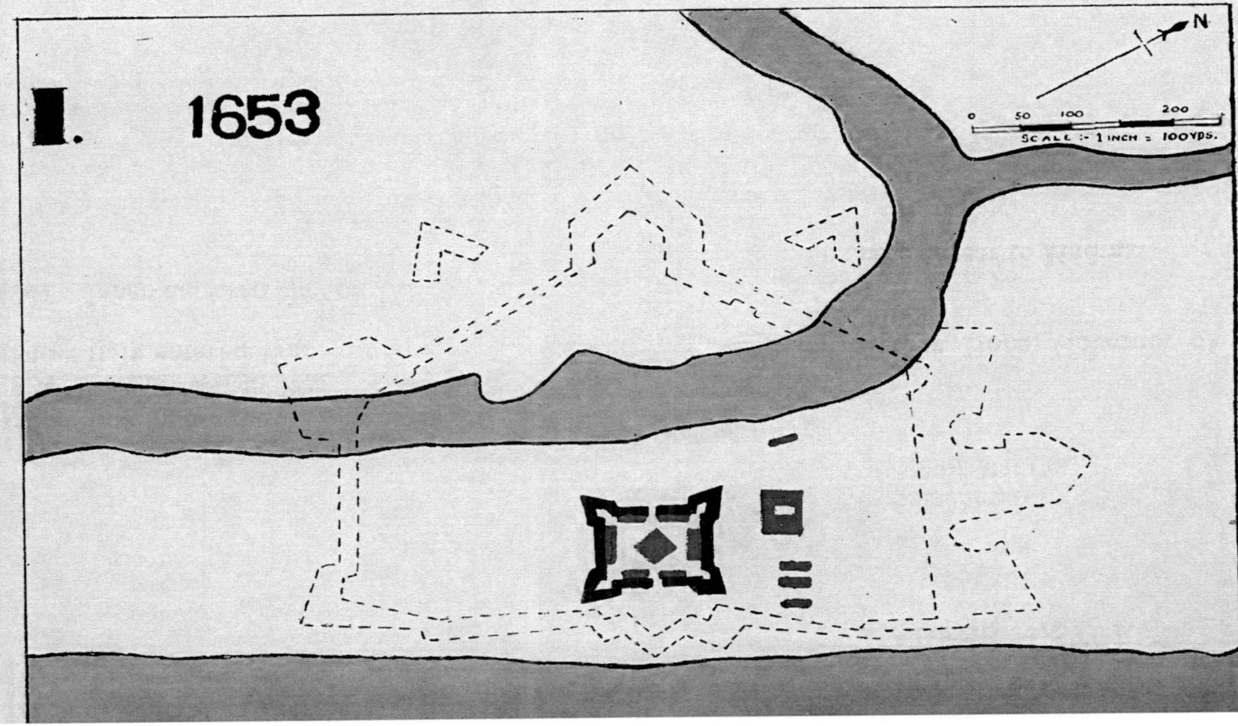
I. 1653
N
0 50 100 200
SCALE :- 1 INCH = 100YDS.

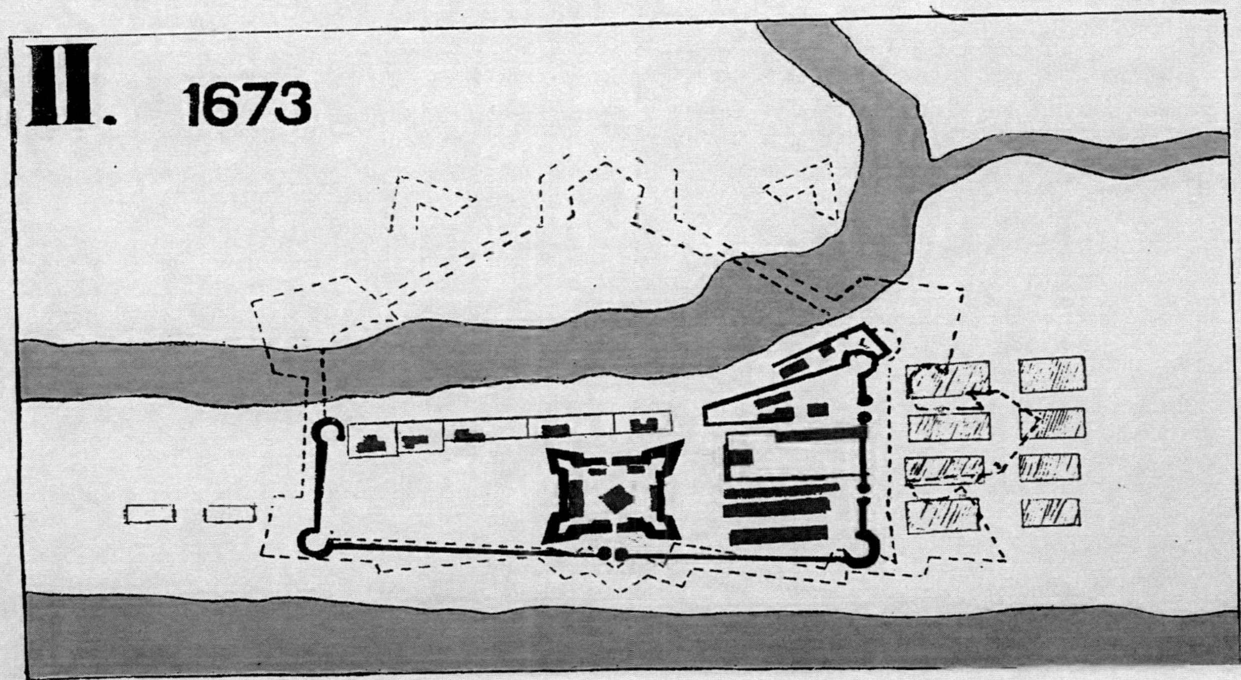
II. 1673

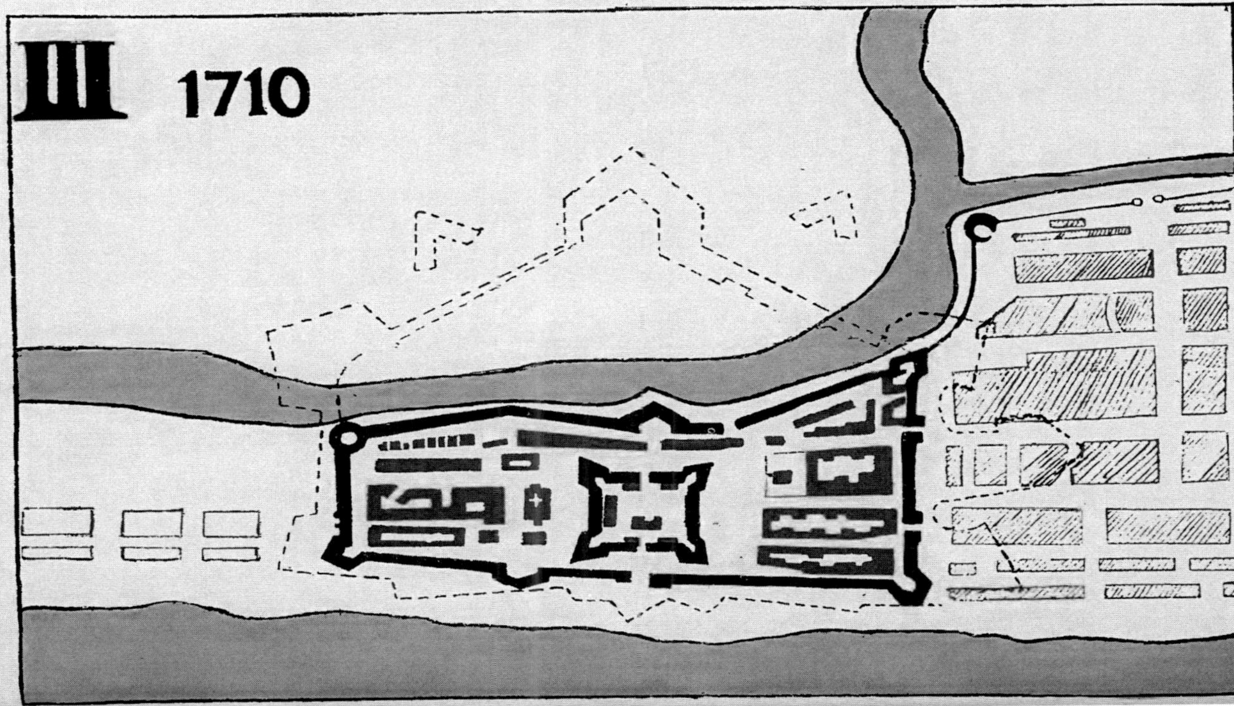
III
1710

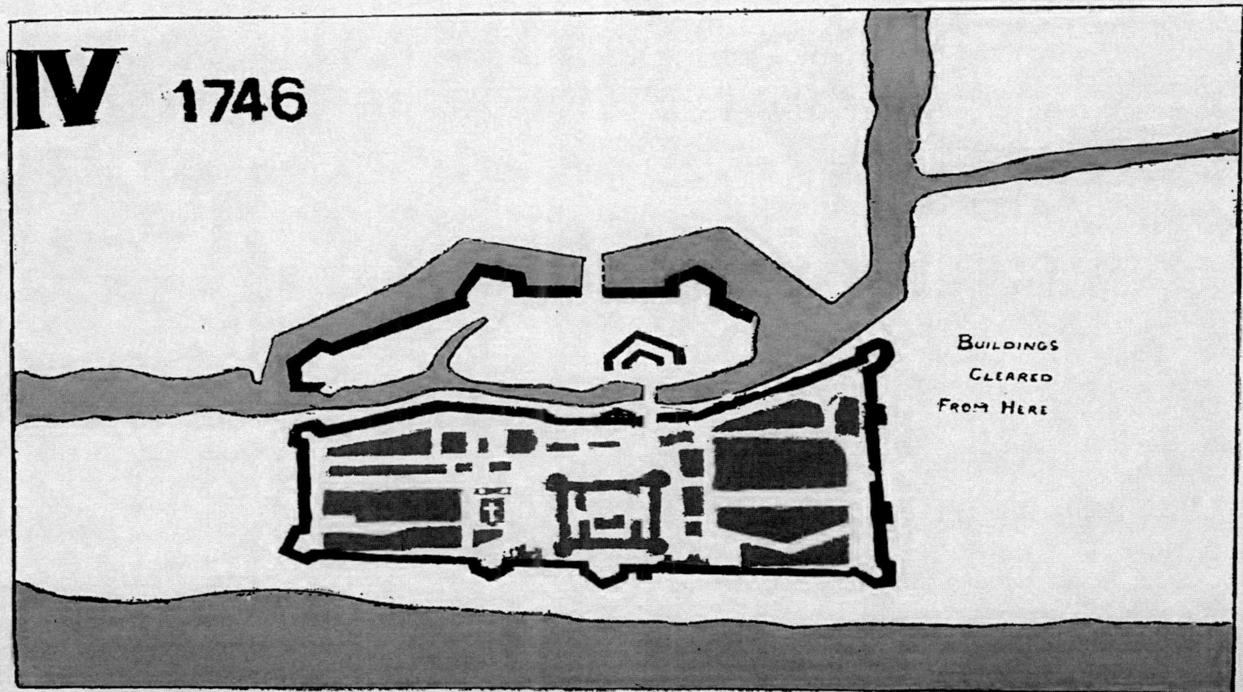
IV 1746
Buildings
Cleared
From Here

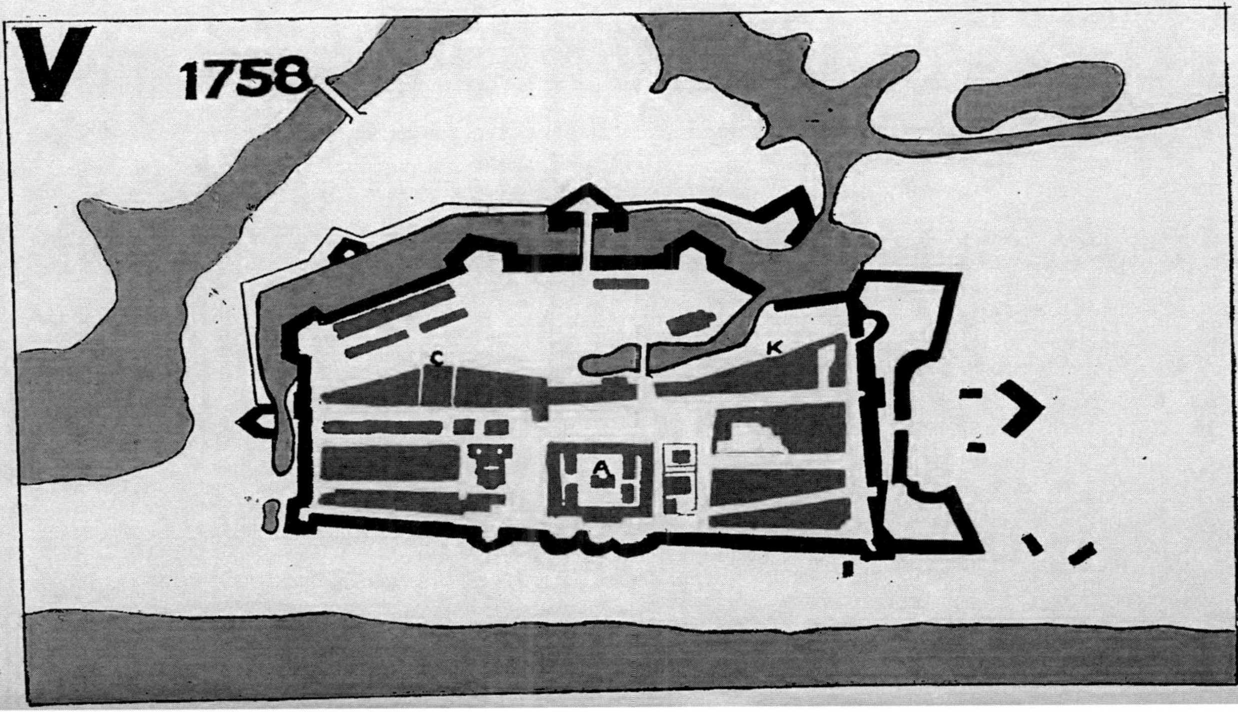
V
1758
C
K
A

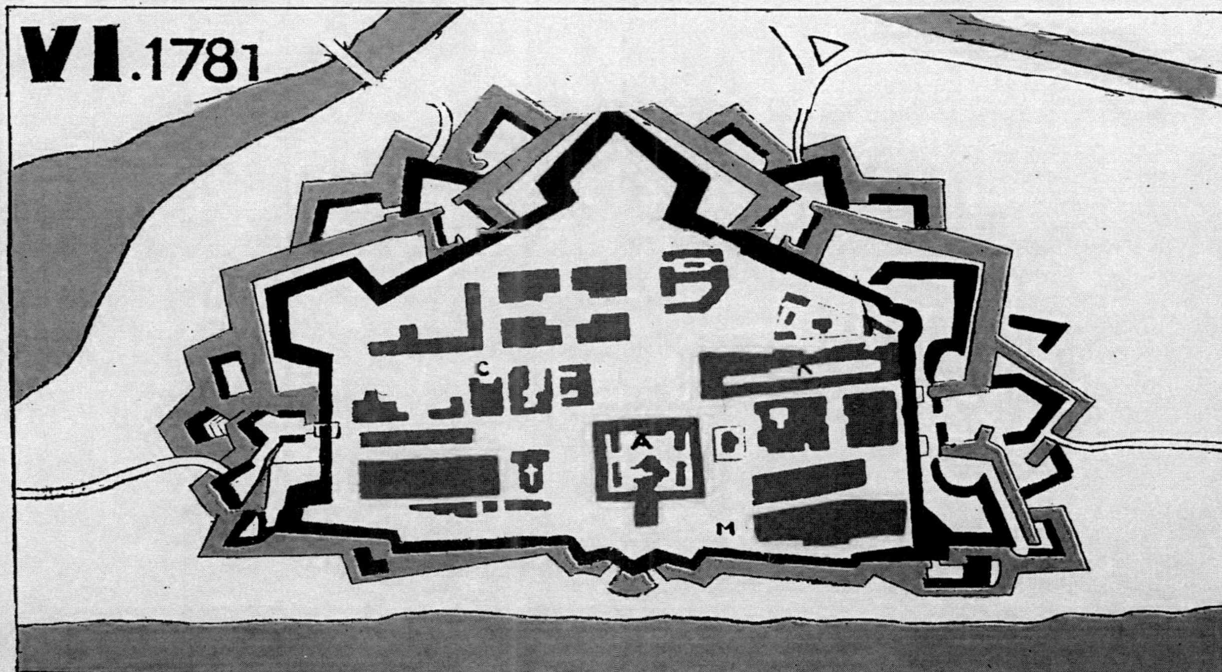
VI.1781
C
A
M

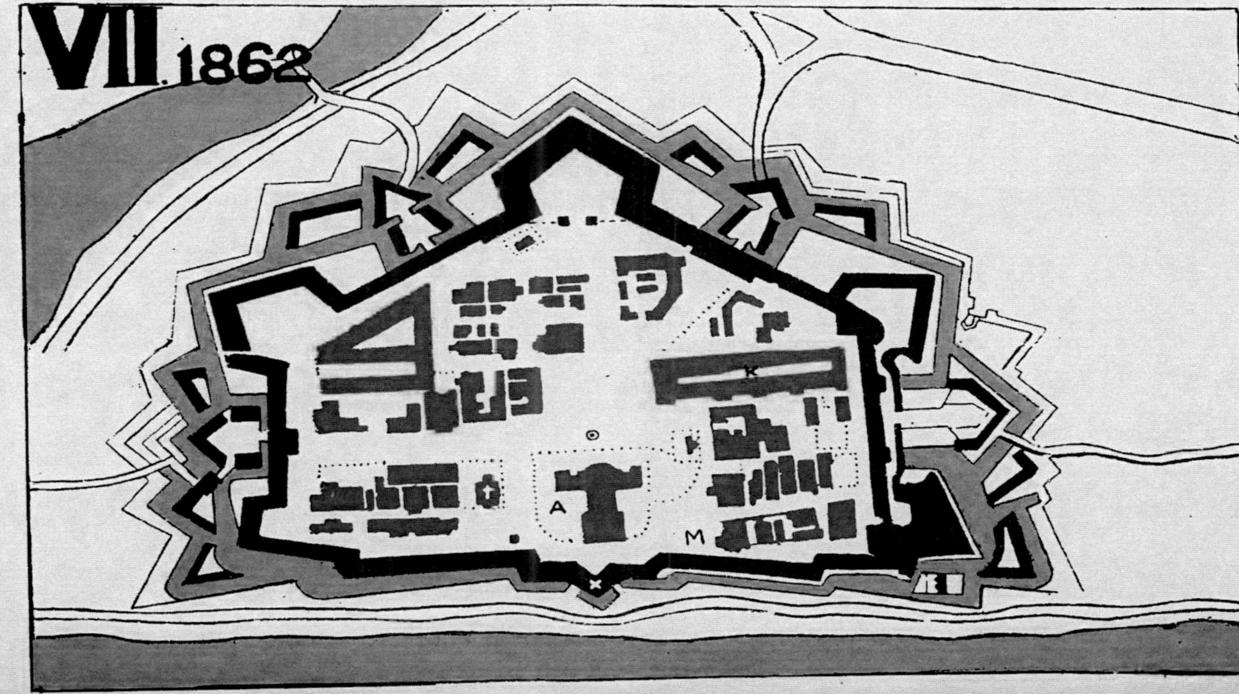
VII.1862
K
A
M

VIII 1939
N
0 50 100
SCALE:- 1 INCH = 10.3 YDS
J
W
C
G
B
Q
K
A
R